A Nature Lovers Guide

California Gardens

Text and Photographs by
Carol Leigh

CAPRA PRESS
SANTA BARBARA

Cover and title page designer: Denise Eltinge
Book designer: Tom Leja
Editor: Annette Burden
Electronic film compositor: In-Color, Santa Barbara

LIBRARY OF CONGRESS CATALOGING-IN-PUBLICATION DATA

Leigh, Carol, 1949-
California gardens: a nature lover's guide / Carol Leigh.
p.   cm.
ISBN 0-88496-337-3
1. Gardens—California—Guidebooks. 2. Garden fauna—California—
Guidebooks.   I. Title
SB466.U65C24   1993
712'.5' 09794—dc20   92-45277
                                                        CIP

CAPRA PRESS
Post Office Box 2068
Santa Barbara, CA 93120

Dedicated to my husband, Chris Smith,
who never doubts, who always sees the possibilities,
and is ever enthusiastic:
and to Michael Cardwell,
who's been there from the beginning.

CAROL LEIGH is a San Francisco–based writer/photographer whose photographs appear in magazines, books and newspapers. She's the co–author of *Photographer's Guide to California* and *Photographers Guide to Los Angeles.*

TABLE OF CONTENTS

GARDENS OF SOUTHERN CALIFORNIA

Antelope Valley California Poppy Reserve, *Lancaster*

Anza-Borrego Desert State Park, *Borrego Springs*

Botanical Building, *San Diego*

Descanso Gardens, *La Cañada-Flintridge*

Desert Garden, *San Diego*

Fullerton Arboretum, *Fullerton*

Grigsby Cactus Gardens, *Vista*

Hortense Miller Garden, *Laguna Beach*

Huntington Botanical Gardens, *San Marino*

Inez Grant Parker Memorial Rose Garden, *San Diego*

The Living Desert, *Palm Desert*

Los Angeles State and County Arboretum, *Arcadia*

Mildred E. Mathias Botanical Gardens, *Los Angeles*

Mission San Diego de Alcala, *San Diego*

Moorten Botanical Garden, *Palm Springs*

Naiman Tech Center, *San Diego*

Quail Botanical Gardens, *Encinitas*

Rancho Santa Ana Botanic Garden, *Claremont*

Rogers Gardens, *Corona del Mar*

San Diego Wild Animal Park, *Escondido*

San Diego Zoo, *San Diego*

Sherman Library and Gardens, *Corona del Mar*

South Coast Botanic Garden, *Palos Verdes*

University of California, Irvine Arboretum, *Irvine*

University of California, Riverside Botanic Gardens, *Riverside*

Virginia Robinson Gardens, *Beverly Hills*

Wrigley Memorial and Botanical Garden, *Santa Catalina Island*

San Diego Zoo
San Diego

Do no dishonour to the earth lest you dishonour the spirit of man. — HENRY BESTON

HE SPECTACULAR attractions with their sensational names get all the attention: Gorilla Tropics, Tiger River, the Sun Bear Forest. But complementing this huge collection of animals is an even larger botanical collection of 6,000 species. The San Diego Zoo takes justifiable pride in exhibiting both animals and the environment in an informative, aesthetically pleasing, and entertaining manner.

Ranging from 100-foot-tall eucalyptus trees (the zoo's oldest botanical specimens) to an exotic orchid collection, to a spectacular springtime display of jacaranda trees, the well-labeled plants, shrubs, trees, and flowers make up the stage on which the "star" animals are presented.

Garden Highlights

Ficus Collection

Four impressive fig specimens anchor the four corners of the flamingo lagoon, located just inside the zoo entrance. *Ficus nekbudu*, a Kaffir fig from tropical Africa, joins company with *F. watkinsiana* from east Australia. A Moreton Bay fig (*F. macrophylla*), an Australian banyan that grows to 200 feet in the wild, grows near *F. elastica*, an Indian rubber tree from Nepal. Ficus grow throughout the zoo, including *F. religiosa*, also known as the bo tree or sacred fig. It is said that Buddha received his enlightenment while meditating under this species. You can see the *F. religiosa* growing at the top of Bear Canyon. Shell ginger (*Alpinia zerumbei*) blooms here in September.

Waterfowl Pond

The migratory duck pond pools have been converted to a water plant habitat to conserve water. Instead of 66,000 gallons of water being drained once a week, the ponds are now drained once a year. Cannas, water irises, and other plants help to keep the water clean along with fish such as gambusia and catfish, crayfish, and water snails. A princess tree (*Paulownia tomentosa*) blooms with white flower spikes in September, while a nearby flowering hawthorn (*Crataegus* sp.) blooms with clusters of white flowers in May.

Orchids thrive at the San Diego Zoo.

Hummingbird Aviary

Lush plantings create a jungle atmosphere in this small walkthrough aviary. If you can wrest your eyes from the colorful birds (sometimes difficult to do as they whiz past your ears or attempt to pick fuzz off your sweater), you'll see plantings of *Justicia aurea* with reddish yellow tubular blossoms from Mexico and Central America. *Hechtia*, or desert bromeliads, grow near the orange-blooming comb flower plant (*Combretum fruiticosum*) and batwing passionflowers (*Passiflora coriacea*).

Fern Canyon

One of the most beautiful botanical areas in the zoo, Fern Canyon recreates a rain forest environment by means of an aerial misting system in the treetops and humidity from a man-made stream. Jacarandas (*Jacaranda mimosifolia*) from northwest Argentina and naked coral trees (*Erythrina coralloides*) create a shady canopy where morning glories (*Ipomoea tricolor*) with delicate blue-purple flowers sprawl and twine. False bird of paradise (*Heliconia latispatha*) from southern Mexico blooms with bright orange "lobster claw" flowers amid exotic palms, cream ginger (*Hedychium flavum*), bromeliads, honeysuckle fuchsia (*Fuchsia triphylla*), orchids, and ferns.

Tiger River Trail

This 3.5-acre simulation of a tropical Asian rain forest features over 9,000 plants of 500 species. A fine misting system sends out an eerie, cloudlike vapor every 20 minutes from 8:30 a.m. to 3:00 p.m. daily. The mist lasts five minutes, enough to keep a wide variety of densely planted tropical plants happy. You'll see banana trees (*Musa acuminata zebrina*), bamboo (*Bambusa vulgaris vittata*), orchid trees (*Bauhinia saigonensis*), palms, ginger, and fragrant jasmine along the winding pathway.

Gorilla Tropics

Inside this lavishly planted and well-marked exhibit, gorillas enthusiastically munch on *Hibiscus rosasinensia* and use bamboo for tools or toys. Outside the exhibit you wander past red-flowering spicy jatropha (*Jatropha integerrima*), Puerto Rican royal palms (*Roystonea borinquena*), travelers palms (*Ravenala madagascariensis*), dragon trees from Madagascar (*Dracena marginata*), dark purple *Thunbergia battiscombei,* and gorilla grass (*Aframomum* sp.) rarely seen outside Africa. One area of plantings around Gorilla Tropics, the "Fruit Loop," features trees and shrubs such as tapioca (*Manihot esculenta*) and coffee (*Coffea arabica*) plants. A sausage tree (*Kigelia pinnata*) flanks the lower ramp coming out of Scripps Aviary.

Throughout the Zoo

More than 30 species of coral trees (*Erythrina*) grow throughout the zoo. Most display brilliant red-orange flowers on leafless branches in late winter to early spring. Most aloes—native to Madagascar, Arabia, and Africa—bloom in early winter. At the San Diego Zoo, however, you can find aloes in bloom almost year round, especially *Aloe arborescens* with its bright red blossoms. *A. massawana* blooms sporadically from August to January. In July, look for the pink-flowering *A. bellatula.*

Chorisia speciosa, with its thorny trunk and pink flowers, produces pods the size of a papaya that split open to reveal seeds with silky fibers attached. The zoo's hummingbirds love this material and use it widely in their nests.

The zoo grows many plants specifically to feed to the animals. Banana leaves and fruit are fed to the larger primates, and the trunks are cut up and fed to the elephants. *Musa velutina* bears bright pink fruit and pink-ribbed leaves. Numerous varieties of ginger in Fern Canyon and along Tiger River Trail include fragrant white ginger (*Hedychium coronarium*) and bright yellow-flowering Kahili ginger (*H. gardneranum*).

More than 150 species of eucalyptus help to feed the koalas, who also eat ten fresh-cut pieces of bamboo a day. The lesser pandas require great quantities of leafy bamboo material as well. In a pinch, the zoo can supplement the supply from its 18 species thanks to a list of bamboo donors—people in the Bamboo Society willing to help out in an emergency.

Palms and flowering plants line the zoo's walkways.

Another important plant for animal food, or "browse," is the hibiscus. Over 200 one-foot pieces of hibiscus leaves and flowers a day feed the 14 species of leaf-eating monkeys. The monkeys also enjoy ficus leaves, mulberry, and cup of gold.

The zoo's yellow fever trees (*Acacia xanthophloea*) provide the giraffes' favorite food. Zebras, camels, antelopes, and gazelles also dine on acacia leaves. The Sumatran rhino alone eats over 60 pounds of plant material a day, so anything the zoo can plant and grow on the grounds makes it easier and more economical for feeding the animals.

Location:
In Balboa Park on Park Boulevard.

Hours and Admission:
Open daily from 9:00 a.m. to 5:00 p.m. in the summer, closing at 4:00 p.m. during the rest of the year. Admission fee.

For More Information:
San Diego Zoo
P.O. Box 551
San Diego, CA 92112
(619) 234-3153

Botanical Building
San Diego

In the gleaming water of the sky-blue river,
clouds swim.   — ANNA AKHMATOVA

 RIGINALLY planned as a Santa Fe Railroad station, the Botanical Building's steel framework was instead combined with redwood laths to create a semiclosed environment for tropical and subtropical plants in Balboa Park. A long, wide lily pond, bordered with flowers and filled with water lilies and lotus, leads your eye to the open lattice of the building.

These openwork domes bring the outside in along with an occasional Anna's hummingbird or Abert's towhee. Four king palms anchor each corner and overlook 1,000 permanent and seasonal plants including heliconias, impatiens, cattleya and cymbidium orchids, Tasmanian tree ferns (*Dicksonia antarctica*), begonias, and poinsettias.

Location:
In Balboa Park next to Casa del Prado, just south of the San Diego Zoo.

Hours and Admission:
Open Tuesday through Sunday 10:00 a.m. to 4:00 p.m.; closed January 1, Thanksgiving, and December 25. Admission free.

For More Information:
City of San Diego
Balboa Park Management Center
2130 Pan American Plaza
San Diego, CA 92101
(619) 525-8200

Desert Garden
San Diego

Nature will bear the closest inspection. She invites us to lay our eye level with her smallest leaf, and take an insect view of its plain.

—THOREAU

 HE DESERT GARDEN surprises you twice. Once, because you probably didn't know it was there; again, because it's so deceptively large. It may look small from the road as you drive up and park your car, but its 2.5 acres hold over 1,200 plants on its perch above Florida Canyon. Often overlooked by people intent on visiting the San Diego Zoo, the garden is usually empty, its quiet broken only by passenger planes landing at nearby Lindbergh Field.

Featuring mostly succulents, aloes, and agaves, the garden is at its showiest from January through May. Brilliant magenta iceplant flowers dazzle you as they swarm across rounded knolls. The candlelike orange blossoms of aloes and the coral trees (*Erythrina*) that bloom in March send their colors up and out—beautiful against a deep blue sky.

Paved pathways wind from barrel cactus to jade plant to redblooming ocotillo. A palm grove with cool, gray-green fronds provides a shady respite from the Southern California sun.

Mockingbirds balance on top of aloe blooms, Anna's hummingbirds routinely zip through the garden, lizards scurry across the paths, and red-tailed hawks sometimes soar overhead.

Mockingbird on aloe.

The Desert Garden comes alive in spring.

Location:
In Balboa Park on the east side of Park Boulevard, just south of the San Diego Zoo.

Hours and Admission:
Open from dawn to dusk. Admission free.

For More Information:
City of San Diego
Balboa Park Management Center
2130 Pan American Plaza
San Diego, CA 92101
(619) 525-8200

Inez Grant Parker Memorial Rose Garden

San Diego

The desert shall rejoice, and blossom as the
rose. — BIBLE, JEREMIAH 35:1

 HIS GARDEN is a perfect complement to its neighbor, the Desert Garden. When the roses are at their showiest, the Desert Garden takes a backseat. And when the Desert Garden blooms (January through March), there isn't a rose to be found next door. The garden is especially peaceful on a cool morning in late summer as you stand beneath a pergola covered with Lady Banks' roses and overlook Florida Canyon east to the mountains.

Dedicated to Inez Grant Parker in 1975, the garden packs 2,000 rose bushes into its 1.25 acres. Curved raised beds that circle a fountain and the pergola feature All-America Rose Selections, floribundas, and hybrid teas.

Location:
In Balboa Park on the east side of Park Boulevard, just south of the San Diego Zoo.

Hours and Admission:
Open daily from dawn to dusk. Admission free.

For More Information:
City of San Diego
Balboa Park Management Center
2130 Pan American Plaza
San Diego, CA 92101
(619) 525-8200

Dew-covered rose in San Diego.

Mission San Diego de Alcala

San Diego

I should like to enjoy this summer flower by flower, as if it were to be the last one for me.

— ANDRE GIDE

 HE FIRST of California's chain of missions, Mission San Diego's most striking architectural feature is a brilliant white campanile containing five large bells. Behind this bell tower is a quiet, shady little pocket of cool green jade plants, purple bougainvillea, pink and white camellias and azaleas, tall tree ferns, pots of begonias, and clumps of orange-spiked aloes. Tile walkways lead you around the garden.

A sunny strip in the courtyard next to the chapel is planted with various cacti and succulents such as candle cactus, teddy bear cholla (*Opuntia bigelovii*), and prickly pear. Large pepper trees (*Schinus molle*) surround the traditional fountain in the main courtyard. Relax on one of the benches next to the fountain, and you immediately smell the sharp tang of pepper.

Location:
In eastern San Diego on San Diego Mission Road.

Hours and Admission:
Open daily from 9:00 a.m. to 5:00 p.m.; closed Thanksgiving and December 25. Modest admission fee.

For More Information:
Mission San Diego de Alcala
10818 San Diego Mission Road
San Diego, CA 92108-2498
Visitor Center: (619) 281-8449

Naiman Tech Center
San Diego

*Do not the most moving moments of our lives
find us all without words?* — MARCEL MARCEAU

 HE JAPANESE garden at the Naiman Tech Center is so secluded you really have to search to find it. The secluded feeling continues inside the garden—the only sounds you hear are the constant rush of water and an occasional jet taking off from nearby Miramar Naval Air Station.

Tucked behind a modern office complex, this little garden's most beautiful feature is a pond with waterfalls, stone lanterns, and koi. A Japanese restaurant perches next to the pond, with outdoor tables and chairs so you can enjoy the view as you eat.

Both the restaurant and pond nestle in a little hollow. Rising up around you are green hillsides where, in spring, azaleas dot the greenery with patches of bright red and pink. The pond is bordered on one side with lush green bamboo, the other side with cedars and redwoods. Enormous koi in patterns of red, orange, black, and white glide slowly through the water, while Anna's hummingbirds—iridescent flashes of green and red—hover over the surface. Common yellowthroats flit from branch to branch; black phoebes dart out from their favorite perches from time to time; and snowy egrets often wait patiently high on a tree limb or stalk their prey next to the pond's edge.

The rest of the gardens consist of large, mounded grassy areas broken by winding stone pathways lined with azaleas and other shrubs.

Location:

Ten miles northeast of downtown San Diego off Mira Mesa Boulevard. Turn left at Scranton Road where you see the huge red sculpture.

Hours and Admission:
Open daily from dawn to dusk. Admission free.

For More Information:
Naiman Tech Center
9605 Scranton Road
San Diego, CA 92121
(619) 453-9550

Enormous koi fill the pond at Naiman Tech Center.

Quail Botanical Gardens
Encinitas

Although I appreciate formal gardens, I would rather be in a place such as Quail that's informally planned. You feel you're out there with nature. — DOCENT AT QUAIL BOTANICAL GARDENS

UAIL Botanical Gardens began as a 25-acre parcel of land donated in 1957 by Ruth Baird Larabee. Two years later the gardens were designated a unit of the San Diego County Parks and Recreation Department.

Small enough to be intimate yet large enough to display a wide variety of trees, plants, flowers, ponds, and streams, the gardens roll and meander through canyons and up hillsides, in and out of sun and shade, with the constant rushing sound of a waterfall in the background. Self-guiding trails surprise you with a tropical rain forest at one turn, sunny desert slopes at another.

Garden Highlights

Flowers and Plants

The Mildred Macpherson Waterfall and Palm Canyon form the gardens' centerpiece, surrounded on all sides by plantings broken into geographical divisions such as the North American, South African, Himalayan, and Australian sections and Desert, Old-Fashioned, Subtropical Fruit, and Bamboo gardens.

The Mildred Macpherson Waterfall slices down a palm and cycad canyon, terminating in a number of small pools. Australian tree ferns, king and queen palms, philodendrons, Mexican palms (*Sabal mexicana*), banana trees (*Ensete ventricosum*), and

Ross Estey hibiscus.

bromeliads follow the waterfall's course to create a tropical atmosphere along the canyon. A spectacular Kashmir cypress (*Cupressus cashmeriana*) grows at the waterfall overlook, inviting you to stroke its soft gray-green needles.

Water lilies, angel's trumpet (*Brugmansia*), orange- and yellow-flowered marmalade bush (*Streptosolen jamesonii*), and Mexican fountain bush (*Russelia equisetiformis*) cluster in and around the pools. The dark purple flowers of *Thunbergia battiscombei* add to the tropical atmosphere.

Ranunculi bloom
at Quail
Botanical Gardens.

The Old-Fashioned Garden, with its arbor, birdbath, and seasonal flowers, is the most colorful garden and yet is very tranquil. The focal point is a large Noisette rose tree, where you can sit on a bench, smell the flowers, and watch the sun glint off the ocean a mile west.

The South African section contains an extensive protea collection. Named for the Greek sea god Proteus, who could assume a variety of shapes, protea flowers range from waxy, orange-tentacled blooms the size of tennis balls to red and gray furry heads as big as cantaloupes.

In the Desert Gardens, a tall, slender organ-pipe cactus (*Lemaireocereus marginata*) grows next to an oddly shaped elephant tree (*Pachycormus discolor*). A big clump of spurge, *Euphorbia canariensis*, sits grandly amid numerous varieties of aloe and a few delicate-leaved acacia trees. The Desert Gardens are especially lovely January through May, when aloes raise their colorful blooms, followed by cactus flowers in shades of orange, yellow, and magenta.

Birds

Birders regularly visit the garden, hoping to spot the two coveys of California quail (*Callipepla californica*) that live there. One covey can be seen across the parking lot near the Ecke Building; the other lives in the Himalayan section. Look for roadrunners

Tropical species cluster by the side of a little pond.

in the native plant area of the North American section. Acorn woodpeckers (laughing maniacally) fly among the cork oaks. Other birds include bushtits, wrentits, mourning doves, Anna's hummingbirds, brown towhees, mockingbirds, western king-birds, hermit thrushes, ravens, and red-shouldered hawks. Small flocks of cedar waxwings sometimes swoop through in winter.

Animals

The animals living at Quail Botanical Gardens are pretty shy. But if you're lucky, you may spot a coyote or a gray fox very early in the morning in the North American section. Ground squirrels, raccoons, opossums, brush rabbits, skunks, gophers, and mice live throughout the gardens. You may see salamanders along the waterway and around the ponds. Lizards scurry through the underbrush and sun themselves on rocks just about everywhere, especially in the Desert Garden.

Insects

Quail Botanical Gardens is slowly becoming a regular habitat for monarch butterflies (*Danaus plexippus*). According to a garden spokesperson, happy to see the orange and black butterflies roosting in the gardens, "Last year they set themselves up in the Torrey pines by the waterfall. They seem to like the atmosphere and humidity."

Tours

Free guided tours begin each Saturday morning at 10:00 a.m. Docents, who complete an eight-week training program and spend at least eight hours a month in the gardens, take you through the different sections. They'll undoubtedly show you the shimmering silver tree (*Leucadendron argenteum*), whose soft furry leaves lend a metallic effect to Rose Parade floats each year. The first Tuesday of the month at 10:30 a.m. is set aside for children's tours. Accompanied by parents or teachers, children from 2 to 12 years of age enjoy tours specifically geared to their age group and/or school studies.

Location:
A half-mile east on Encinitas Boulevard past the exit of Interstate 5, then north on Quail Gardens Drive.

Hours and Admission:
Open daily from 8:00 a.m. to 5:00 p.m. Admission free; parking $1.

For More Information:
Quail Botanical Gardens
230 Quail Gardens Drive
P.O. Box 5
Encinitas, CA 92024
(619) 436-3036

San Diego Wild Animal Park

Escondido

As for the Future, your task is not to foresee, but to enable it. — ANTOINE DE SAINT-EXUPERY

HERE AREN'T MANY GARDENS where you have to walk past the cheetahs to get to the flowers! The San Diego Wild Animal Park, while noted for its extensive animal collection, features an even more extensive botanical collection. Throughout the park you'll pass by various plantings of geraniums, eucalyptus trees, bromeliads, fuchsias, and palms. In addition, a number of separate gardens feature 110 species of aloes, 90 species of Baja California plants, 600 species of epiphyllums, and 75 species of herbs.

Epiphyllum.

Garden Highlights

Baja Garden

This garden houses the most extensive collection of Baja California cacti in the world, including some endangered species. One of the stranger plants is the boojum tree (*Indria columnaris*), growing next to a candelilla (*Pedilanthus macrocarpa*). Dirt pathways lead between barrel cactus, beavertail cactus (*Opuntia basilaris*), and agave (*Maguey shawii*). Here and in the Native Plant Garden you'll see purple finches, hooded orioles, rufous-sided towhees, black-chinned hummingbirds, phainopeplas, roadrunners, turkey vultures, and ravens.

Native Plant Garden

Adjacent to the Baja Garden grow native California plants such

An agave *(Maguey shawii)*
in full bloom.

as the island tree poppy (*Dendromecon rigida harfordii*), summer holly (*Comarostaphyllis diversifolia*), matilija poppy (*Romneya coulteri*), and orange monkey-flower (*Diplacus aurantiacus*). Western jimsonweed (*Datura wrightii*), whose white trumpet flowers look like morning glories on steroids, drapes itself over the rocks. Joshua trees, California poppies, and brass buttons (*Cotula coronopifolia*) grow along the pathways.

Bonsai House

Handsome displays of miniaturized trees (an art form in Japan for more than 1,000 years) include a California juniper (*Juniperus californica* San Jose) and a pomegranate with bright orange flowers (*Punica granatum*). Informative signs and pamphlets enhance viewer appreciation and enjoyment.

Epiphyllum House

Visit the Epiphyllum House in spring to fully appreciate the grandeur of these iridescent flowers, some as large as dinner plates. Also known as "leaf cactus," epiphytes grow on trees in the wild, gathering nourishment from rain and air rather than from their hosts. Here they hang in pots at eye level in a shady enclosure.

Herb Garden

Elephant garlic (*Allium ampeloprasum*), society garlic (*Tulbaghia violaceae*), and white rosemary (*Rosmarinus officinalis*) grow in a small herb garden near the cheetahs. *Iris florentina* adds color.

Protea Garden

A pathway leading to the Protea Garden features a number of coastal plants, including Catalina ironwood (*Lyonothamnus floribundus*) from Santa Catalina Island, Torrey pines, and flannelbush. Over 42 species of protea include the showy banksia (*Banksia speciosa*) and the treelike acorn banksia (*B. prionotes*).

Egrets gather near the Mombasa Pavilion.

African Marsh

Islands in a big pond near the Mombasa Pavilion are packed in springtime with great egrets—spectacular in their seasonal plumage. In addition to coots, cormorants, and great blue herons, the marsh attracts southern white pelicans, ringed teal, cape teal (*Anas capensis*), black-crowned night herons, red-winged blackbirds, and white-faced whistling ducks (*Dendrocygna viduata*).

Location:
Five miles east of Interstate 5's Rancho Parkway exit.

Hours and Admission:
Open daily from 9:00 a.m. to 6:00 p.m., closing at 4:00 p.m. after Labor Day till mid-June. Admission fee.

For More Information:
San Diego Wild Animal Park
Rt. 1, Box 725 E
Escondido, CA 92025
(619) 234-6541

Grigsby Cactus Gardens
Vista

Nature has fram'd strange fellows in her time.
— WILLIAM SHAKESPEARE

DAVID GRIGSBY'S collection of succulents and cacti spread out over 3.5 acres of greenhouses, plots, and terraces. Specializing in rare and fancy items, the garden sells plants to nurseries and the public. This is where you can find the rare *Aloe suzannae* from Madagascar; *Aloe thraskii*, the national flower of Zimbabwe; and the bizarre root-above-the-ground *Trichodiadema bulbosum*. Grigsby is happy to point out his personal favorites and some of the rarer of the plants.

Ask for the garden catalog ($2), which, in addition to black and white photos, contains delightful descriptions. *Sedum multiceps:* "an utterly charming little fellow that looks much like a miniature Joshua tree." *Sulcorebutia flavissima:* "honey-gold spines and bright rose flowers. What a fabulous combination!" *Senecio pendula:* a "weird plant that acts like a worm growing into the ground and back out again. Fascinating."

This garden provides a little bit of heaven for the cactus and succulent fan and a good education for the novice. As you wander around the grounds, you may spot turkey vultures and hawks flying overhead and hummingbirds attracted to any aloes in bloom.

Cacti bloom in Grigsby greenhouse.

Location:
Off Interstate 5 at the Vista exit (State Route 78) and east to Sycamore. Northeast on Sycamore, right on Santa Fe (S14), left on Palmyra, and right to Bella

Vista Drive. Pull up to the gate and honk for admission.

Hours and Admission:
Open Tuesday through Saturday from 8:00 a.m. to 4:00 p.m.
Admission free.

For More Information:
Grigsby Cactus Garden
2354 Bella Vista Drive
Vista, CA 92084
(619) 727-1323

Anza-Borrego Desert State Park
Borrego Springs

The stars speak of man's insignificance in the long eternity of time; the desert speaks of his insignificance right now. — EDWIN WAY TEALE

 ITH such a variety of terrain, flora, and fauna, Anza-Borrego attracts visitors for a variety of reasons. From waterfalls after a rain to sandstone formations, badlands, oases, and dry washes, the park offers a constantly changing panorama. There are new and different things to discover every time you visit.

Garden Highlights
Wild Flowers
March and April are the peak months to see wild flowers. After a wet winter they can take your breath away with their extravagant lushness and color. Ocotillo (*Fouquieria splendens*), with its clusters of red flowers on long curving stems, is the most obvious—it looks like a fountain of fireworks. Less obvious, but

enchanting nevertheless, is purple mat (*Nama demissum*) with its tiny dark pink flowers creeping across the desert floor. In bold contrast are the bright yellow, orange, and pink flowers of beavertail cactus (*Opuntia basilaris*), jumping cholla (*O. bigelovii*), and barrel cactus (*Echinocactus acanthodes*). Sunny yellow blooms of the desert dandelion (*Malacothrix glabrata*) pop up all over the place.

If you would like to be notified of the peak wild flower bloom, enclose a postcard, stamped and self-addressed, in an envelope addressed to Wildflowers, P.O. Box 299, Borrego Springs, CA 92004. The card will be mailed back to you two weeks before the expected peak bloom.

Birds

Although wild flowers are the main attraction in spring, Anza-Borrego Desert State Park is a major draw for birders as well. Gambel's quail (*Callipepla gambelii*), with distinctive black breast patches, scurry through the desert scrub gently calling to one another from March through August. California quail (*C. californica*) live in the chaparral all year. Sleek phainopeplas (*Phainopepla nitens*), looking like shiny black blue jays, live here year round and tend to congregate in and around the marshes and ponds.

The wetter areas also attract bright orange and black hooded orioles and Scott's orioles from March through August. Costa's hummingbirds flit around the ocotillo blossoms from March through May. You can see red-tailed hawks and roadrunners (reaching speeds up to 30 miles per hour) all year, white-throated swifts from March through August, northern flickers year round (except June through August), and ladder-backed woodpeckers in the desert scrub.

The Anza-Borrego Desert Natural History Association publishes a birding checklist, available for purchase in the headquarters gift shop. They especially recommend Lower Willows in Coyote Canyon, Yaqui Well, Agua Caliente (for white-winged doves), Vallecito, and Borrego Palm Canyon as excellent birding spots. Also check at headquarters for the schedule of bird-watching tours.

Animals and Reptiles

Daylight hours are for the birds and hardier creatures such as western fence lizards, flat-tailed horned lizards, Sonoran gopher snakes, and red diamond rattlesnakes. At dusk and dawn look for kangaroo rats, coyotes, black-tailed jackrabbits, kit foxes, and gray foxes. Anza-Borrego Desert State Park is also home to bighorn sheep. Bring your binoculars to scan the hillsides above Tamarisk Grove Campground. Although they normally live at higher elevations, the sheep occasionally come down from the mountains during dry periods and have been seen drinking amid the fan palms at the spring in Borrego Palm Canyon.

Ocotillos bloom everywhere at Anza-Borrego Desert State Park.

Location:
Just west of Borrego Springs off Highway 78.

Hours and Admission:
Open daily October through May from 9:00 a.m. to 5:00 p.m. Open June through September from 9:00 a.m. to 5:00 p.m. only on weekends, July 4, and Labor Day. Admission free to wander around the Visitor Center. Day use fee applies to hikers using the trails emanating from numerous campgrounds.

For More Information:
Anza-Borrego Desert State Park
P.O. Box 299
Borrego Springs, CA 92004
Recorded park information: (619) 767-4684
Administrative office: (619) 767-5311

Moorten
Botanical Garden
Palm Springs

*Take your time like a turtle, and you will see
more.* — GARDEN SIGN

 HERE'S a certain casualness and nonchalance about
this garden that makes it quite charming. It begins
with the hand-drawn map you're given at the front
entrance. The map guides you to the Tortoise Ter-
race, pioneer relics, and through four acres containing more
than 2,000 plant varieties.

Arranged in regional sections, the plants are well-marked and
displayed along a circular pathway through the grounds. Organ-
pipe cactus and a boojum tree grow next to Joshua trees, barrel

A casual hodgepodge of well-marked desert plants.

cactus, and beavertail cactus. A wide variety of cacti grow inside the world's first "cactarium," visited from time to time by Anna's hummingbirds and common ground doves. Cactus wrens and ground doves nest in some of the garden cacti—the ground doves often right at eye level.

Begun in 1938 around the residence of Patricia and "Cactus Slim" Moorten, the gardens (also known as "Desertland") continue on in the hands of their son Clark.

Location:
On the south end of Palm Springs where South Palm Canyon Drive turns to become East Palm Canyon Drive.

Hours and Admission:
Open Monday through Saturday from 9:00 a.m. to 5:00 p.m., Sunday from 10:00 a.m. to 4:00 p.m. Modest admission fee.

For More Information:
Moorten Botanical Garden
1701 S. Palm Canyon Drive
Palm Springs, CA 92264
(619) 327-6555

The Living Desert
Palm Desert

Come forth into the light of things, Let Nature be your teacher. — WILLIAM WORDSWORTH

 OUNDED in 1970 by Philip Boyd as a 360-acre wilderness preserve, the Living Desert has expanded into 1,200 acres of education, conservation, and research related to the desert environment.

From the main entrance you can take trails to exhibits of animals including desert bighorn sheep, Arabian oryxes, Grevy's zebras, gazelles, and meerkats. Or you can take the pathways that wind through an extensive botanical garden. Twelve hundred acres and six miles of nature trails are a lot of ground to cover—way too much for a single day. More than 7,000 individual plants—more than 1,500 desert species—form the most comprehensive collection in Southern California.

Garden Highlights

Plants and Flowers

Paths through the botanical garden guide you past the Euphorbia and Cactus gardens, a prairie falcon exhibit, and into the various desert regions. Feathery palo verde plants blend well with mesquite (*Prosopis chilensis*) and desert ironwood (*Olneya tesota*) in the Sonoran Garden. An impressive collection of opuntia cacti, including *Opuntia linguiformis* (cow's tongue) and *O. basilaris* (beavertail cactus), flourish in the Opuntia Garden nearby. Palms grow throughout the gardens, including rare blue fan palms (*Brahea armata*).

Butterflies

You're likely to spot a variety of butterflies, particularly painted ladies (*Vanessa cardui*). The most widely distributed butterfly in the world, these orange and black insects feed on nectar from a variety of wild flowers. Pearly marblewings (*Euchloe hyantis*) feed on sagebrush nectar from March through May; their larvae feed on desert alyssum (*Lepidum fremontii*). Desert checkerspots (*Charidryas neumoegeni*)—orange with a few thin, zigzag

black bands—flit about from March through May as well; their larvae feed on desert aster (*Machaeranthera tortifolia*).

Birds

Your walk through the garden will take you past a number of bird displays, including a walk-through aviary and owl, kestrel, and ferruginous hawk exhibits. A large eagle display area called Eagle Canyon is in the works.

Pond, Living Desert.   Lots of wild birds make the Living

Six miles of nature trails wind through the Living Desert.

Desert their home. Costa's hummingbirds frequent the botanical garden along with verdins (check the mesquite shrubs for nests), Abert's towhees (the desert version of a brown towhee), cactus wrens (*Campylorhynchus brunneicapillus*), and black-throated sparrows. A roadrunner may zip past you on the pathway, often with a lizard in its beak.

Location:
Thirteen miles southeast of Palm Springs, a mile past Rancho Mirage.

Hours and Admission:
Open daily September 1 to June 15 from 9:00 a.m. to 4:30 p.m. Admission fee.

For More Information:
Living Desert Reserve
47900 Portola Avenue
Palm Desert, CA 92260
(619) 346-5694

Hortense Miller Garden
Laguna Beach

"Can you climb a ladder?" Thinking this 82-year-old woman needed me to help her with something, I said sure. She scampered up the ladder like a ten-year-old and yelled back at me, "Then come on up! You have a better view from here!"

ORTENSE MILLER was right. The view *was* terrific: the entire garden laid out with the Pacific Ocean glinting in the distance. This private garden enjoys a certain amount of freedom. The untamed, sometimes unruly mass of unusual, often ephemeral plants and flowers reflects the soul, spirit, and intelligence of Miller herself, who began her 2.5-acre garden in 1959 on the slopes of Boat Canyon.

Garden Highlights

Plants and Flowers

Plants range from the exotic to the familiar. Rare blue-flowering *Petrea volubis* sprawls over the roof of the house. Delicate white *Iris florentina* surprises you on the garden path. The blue-green

flowers of *Puya alpestris* take you aback with their dark, sinister beauty. More familiar are narcissus, bougainvillea, Lady Banks' roses, California poppies, and jasmine. Cymbidium orchids appear here and there.

A less flashy but ecologically important area is the garden's drought-resistant chaparral section, with its pungent smell of sage and its sanity-restoring views of undeveloped rolling hillsides. The Pacific shimmers in the distance, ravens fly back

Brilliant pink ice plant in bloom.

and forth to their nest across the canyon, and red-tailed hawks cruise the skies. Flames that raged through the canyon in 1979 spared the Miller home but destroyed the gardens. Garden lovers throughout California donated plants and seeds. Mother Nature, too, donated surprise specimens—plants from seeds long dormant in the ground that were just waiting for a fire to spark them to life.

Birds

Miller feeds the numerous birds in her gardens twice a day. Ravens feast on buttered bread and cat food while quail, white-crowned sparrows, and rufous-sided towhees scrabble for birdseed. Scrub jays swoop down for their peanuts and swoop off again to dine in private. Mockingbirds remain aloof, preferring to sing rather than eat. Anna's hummingbirds drink nectar from blue-violet *Echium fastuosum* blossoms, and mourning doves sip from the pools.

Tours

To visit the garden (and get some good ideas for planning your own), you must make an appointment during normal business hours through the City of Laguna Beach's Department of Parks and Recreation. The city will arrange a mutually convenient time and provide for a knowledgeable guide. A normal tour takes two to three hours, including travel time from City Hall. Wear comfortable shoes—you'll be walking up and down sloping, uneven pathways.

Location:
In Boat Canyon, Laguna Beach.

Hours and Admission:
Open for tours only, Tuesday through Friday and Saturday morning, except on national holidays. Admission free, although you may wish to make a donation to the Friends of the Hortense Miller Garden to keep it all going.

For More Information:
Hortense Miller Garden
P.O. Box 742
Laguna Beach, CA 92652
Department of Parks and Recreation: (714) 497-3311

Sherman Library and Gardens

Corona del Mar

I know a little garden close
Set thick with lily and red rose,
Where I would wander if I might
From dewy dawn to dewy night.

— WILLIAM MORRIS

OU'RE whizzing along Pacific Coast Highway in your car on your way to work. Or the store. The beach. An important meeting. You glimpse red tile, warm adobe walls, bright orange flowers, and a sign. Too fast to read the sign. Looked interesting. You make a mental note to stop someday.

You should! Here on one of the busiest streets in Orange County is a visual and mental treat—an island in the mainstream of coastal life where you leave it all behind for a while, relax, smell the flowers, and unwind.

Covering an entire city block, the gardens are a self-described "museum of living plants" ranging from lush tropicals (ferns, bromeliads, orchids) to cacti and succulents.

You'll wander through the tropical conservatory, past small waterfalls, colorful koi, carnivorous plants, exotic orchids, huge ferns, and waxy red anthuriums. Another pathway takes you through a wisteria-draped arbor, past a small garden of modern roses, a water lily pond, a large rectan-

Tea Garden.

gular pool outlined with dianthus—or marigolds or Iceland poppies—to a small, compact cactus garden with fine examples of barrel cactus, agave, aloe, and organ-pipe cactus.

Established in 1958 through the legacy of Moses Hazeltine "General" Sherman, the gardens and library are dedicated to the study of the Pacific Southwest. Housed in the library are over 5,000 books, pamphlets, and other printed materials containing information ranging from shark fishing to avocado growing.

The signature plant here is the fuchsia, and the Tea Garden is lush with them. Hanging baskets bring all the flowers up to eye level, creating a sea of hot purple and neon magenta. Fuchsias thrive in this moist cool climate just a few blocks from the beach.

Location:
On East Coast Highway, a block south of MacArthur Boulevard.

Hours and Admission:
Open daily from 10:30 a.m. to 4:00 p.m. Admission fee.

For More Information:
Sherman Library and Gardens
2647 East Coast Highway
Corona del Mar, CA 92625
(714) 673-2261.

Rogers Gardens
Corona del Mar

A merry heart doeth good like a medicine.
— BIBLE, PROVERBS 17:22

 OGERS GARDENS is the Disneyland of the plant world. Toy trains run on tracks. Topiary figures loom above you. Flags, lots of color, and beautifully planted flower beds create enough razzle and dazzle to leave you exhausted at the end of your visit. And—as with Disneyland—you always come back for more.

Topiary giraffe looms large at Rogers Gardens.

An exuberant combination retail nursery and tourist attraction, this is *the* place in winter to bring your friends from the northeast to gloat about Southern California's perfect weather. The colors are blinding, with hanging baskets of pink and red geraniums, purple and white petunias, and bright yellow marigolds. Little hillsides, planted with wedge-shaped flower beds, erupt with a massive display of California poppies in springtime.

Anyone in the area, whether interested in gardening or not, should take the opportunity to visit this spectacular nursery. It brings out a little of the child in everyone.

Location:
On San Joaquin Hills Road near the intersection of San Joaquin Hills Road.

Hours and Admission:
Open daily from 10:00 a.m. to 4:00 p.m. Admission free.

For More Information:
Rogers Gardens
2301 San Joaquin Hills Road
Corona del Mar, CA 92625
(714) 640-5800

University of California, Irvine Arboretum

Irvine

*Now the smallest creatures, who do not know
    they have names,
In fields of pure sunshine open themselves and
    sing.* — ANNE PORTER

 SAW one of the most relaxed rabbits I've ever seen at this arboretum. He was sprawled in the dirt, taking a dust bath in the warm sun. This was my first visit to the garden, and, based on this rabbit, I knew it would be a fine and leisurely place to wander.

The arboretum's ten acres sprawl over large lawns with pathways open to views of the surrounding campus and nearby San Joaquin Freshwater Marsh. A large stand of palms, looking much like an oasis, grows at one corner of the garden. Lower-growing plants such as aloe (more than 140 species) and agave, iris, lily, and amaryllis appear in beds throughout. Particularly known for its flowering bulbs, the garden blooms with ixias, gladiolas, and watsonias from late February into early March.

The variety of trees punctuating the grounds includes thorny giraffe acacia (*Cassia erioloba*), floss silk trees, coral trees (*Erythrina*), and jacarandas. You'll see Anna's hum-

**Mourning dove perches
on ocotillo stem.**

mingbirds and a lot of mourning doves and mockingbirds. Look in the palms for an occasional hooded oriole.

Location:
Just south of Jamboree Road on Campus Drive.

Hours and Admission:
Open weekdays from 8:30 a.m. to 3:30 p.m. Admission free.

For More Information:
University of California, Irvine Arboretum
Irvine, CA 92717
(714) 856-5011

Wrigley Memorial and Botanical Garden
Santa Catalina Island

Seas roll to waft me, suns to light me rise;
My footstool Earth, my canopy the skies.
— ALEXANDER POPE

 VISIT to the Wrigley Memorial and Botanical Garden might seem almost anticlimactic after traveling 26 miles across the sea, jouncing across a maze of island roads in a little golf cart, and admiring the sweeping vistas of Avalon Harbor.

This lovely botanical garden lies 1.7 miles from downtown Avalon in Avalon Canyon—37 acres of cacti and succulents, aloes, yuccas, and California and Catalina Island native plants. The path takes you up a slight incline to the top of the canyon, past cacti and succulents, aloes, yuccas, and California natives such as bladderpod, Catalina ironwood, Torrey pine, and yellow tree poppies. It culminates in a large memorial to William

Wrigley, Jr., the chewing-gum magnate largely responsible for making Catalina Island the popular resort it is today.

Garden Highlights

Endemic Plants

The garden takes particular pride in showcasing plants that grow naturally on Catalina Island and nowhere else. St. Catherine's lace (*Eriogonum giganteum*), a large buckwheat with silvery green leaves, provides a stunning bit of color in the fall when it turns a deep shade of russet. Catalina live-forever (*Dudleya hassei*) blooms in May and June with star-shaped yellowish white flowers.

California Natives

Clusters of bright red berries decorate toyon, or California holly bushes (*Heteromeles arbutifolia macrocarpa*), from November through January. The pinkish white flowers of lemonade berry (*Rhus integrifolia*) pop out in February and March.

Cacti and Succulents

More spectacular (subjectively speaking) than the endemic and native plants are the varieties of cacti and succulents in the garden. Bluish gray *Euphorbia coerulescens*—a relative of the poinsettia, with poisonous milky white sap—presents a fine example of spurge. Indian fig (*Opuntia ficus-indica*) grows in abundance along with elephant bush (*Portulacaria afra*), a plant favored by elephants in Africa, and dragon-trees (*Dracaena draco*) native to the Canary Islands.

Wrigley Memorial

This imposing building—232 feet wide and 130 feet high—stands at the top of Avalon Canyon overlooking the botanical garden below and the city of Avalon below that. All the decorative tile work, the red tiles on the roof, the blue flagstones on the ramp, and the bright white concrete are natural products of Catalina Island.

Birds

You're likely to see Allen's hummingbirds, northern flickers, rufous-sided towhees, and black phoebes in summer. If you're lucky, you may also find phainopeplas and the northern saw-whet owl. In winter, look for mountain bluebirds, yellow-rumped and orange-crowned warblers, and dark-eyed juncos. If you're even luckier, you may spot bald eagles from the top of Memorial Road, a trail that begins behind the Wrigley Memorial. Even if you don't see any eagles, you'll have an excellent view of Avalon below.

Butterflies

There are three in particular to look for. The Avalon hairstreak (*Strymon avalona*) lives nowhere else in the world. It's a small to medium-sized butterfly, mouse gray on top and slightly lighter gray underneath, with hairlike tails on the hind wings. You'll see it flying on brushy slopes from February to October. The larvae feed on deer weed (*Lotus scoparius*) and silver-leaved trefoil (*L. argophyllum*).

Look also for the Catalina orange-tip (*Anthocharis cethura catalina*), another butterfly that lives only on Santa Catalina Island. March through April is the best time to find it. The larvae feed on mustard and desert candle (*Caulanthus inflatus*).

Gunder's orange-tip (*Anthocharis sara gunderi*) lives both on Santa Cruz Island and Santa Catalina Island. Look for a greenish yellow hind wing and more black markings than a Sara orange-tip. The larvae, like the Catalina orange-tips', feed on mustard.

Location:
At the end of Avalon Canyon Road.

Hours and Admission:
Open daily from 8:00 a.m. to 5:00 p.m. Admission fee.

For More Information:
Wrigley Memorial and Botanical Garden
Wrigley Memorial Garden Foundation
P.O. Box 88
1400 Avalon Canyon Road
Avalon, CA 90704
(213) 510-2288

Fullerton Arboretum
Fullerton

When I've been away from the gardens for a month or a couple of months and come back, I have this feeling of coming home—to a place that I belong to and it belongs to me. It's just a very comfortable feeling being here.

— GARDEN SPOKESPERSON

 NCE an abandoned orange grove, the Fullerton Arboretum is now what it was planned to be, a "green oasis in Orange County's rapidly growing urban area." It's been open since 1979 and gets better as the years go by. The garden's 25 acres hold a variety of plants from around the world, arranged in three major groupings: temperate, tropical, and arid zones. The emphasis is on drought-tolerant plants.

Spring wild flowers at Fullerton Arboretum.

The entrance hints of good things to follow as you pass a small stream and waterfall and an ever-changing array of colorful flowers.

Beavertail cactus.

The most unusual planting in the garden is the Carnivorous Plant Bog, consisting of a number of insect-eating pitcher plants (*Sarracenia*) from around the world growing in a shaded, muddy environment.

Across from the Carnivorous Plant Bog and a small pond stands the ornately designed Heritage House. This 1894 home and office of Fullerton's first physician, Dr. George C. Clark, has been kept up nicely. The Victorian home, with pump house, windmill, old roses, and palm trees, sits behind a tidy white picket fence. The arboretum's Gift and Garden Shop offers books, home accessories, and indoor plants.

Garden Highlights

Temperate Zone

Conifers, redwoods, gingkos, and cycads fill this area with cool green foliage and unusual formations. Of special note is the monkey puzzle tree (*Araucaria araucana*), with its irregularly layered and twisted branches, and the soft, gray-needled Kashmir cypress (*Cupressus cashmeriana*).

Tropical Zone

Plants requiring plenty of water include plumeria, banyan, coral tree, ficus, and the fishtail palm (*Caryota urens*).

Subtropical Area

More drought-tolerant plants, including the Bolivian pink powder puff (*Calliandra haematocephala*), gardenias, and persimmons, flourish in this area. A Thorn Scrub Section features unusual silk floss trees and acacias.

Succulent Garden

If you're looking for color in winter, the succulent garden is a good place to find it. You'll see euphorbias and agaves along with the bright orange candlelike blooms of winter-blooming aloes.

Desert Areas

Spectacular in spring when the cacti and wild flowers bloom, these areas feature a wide variety of *Opuntia* and barrel cacti, yuccas, agaves, and euphorbias.

Mediterranean Region

Cork oaks (*Quercus suber*) provide the main attraction in this section, along with olive and Israeli carob trees.

Foothill Woodland

This is another area of the garden that's fantastic in spring, when the California poppies, yellow monkey-flowers (*Mimulus guttatus*), and baby blue-eyes (*Nemophila menziesii*) all burst into bloom on the slopes.

California Channel Islands

Filled with plants native to the offshore Channel Islands, this section features Catalina ironwood, (*Lyonothamnus floribundus*) and St. Catherine's lace (*Eriogonum giganteum*)—wild buckwheat with big white clusters of flowers.

Deciduous Orchard

You'll find plum, apricot, and nectarine trees, a rose garden, and an arbor draped romantically with pale purple-flowering wisteria. Valencia orange trees are all that remain of the land's former orange grove.

Birds, Reptiles, Amphibians

The little stream you passed on your way into the garden feeds a pond and a small lake, which is where you'll find most of the birds in the garden. Red-winged blackbirds balance precariously on slender reeds in the pond. Mallards, great egrets, and green herons are routinely sighted. Turtles bask in the sunshine. Frogs, heard but rarely seen, startle you as they plop into the water.

Tours

Join an arboretum tour on Sunday at 2:00 p.m. or arrange for a weekday group garden or Heritage House tour by reservation one month in advance. Regular Heritage House tours, with a small fee, are held Sunday from 2:00 to 4:00 p.m. except for the month of August and major holidays.

Location:
At Yorba Linda Boulevard and Associated Road on the campus of California State University at Fullerton.

Hours and Admission:
Open daily from 8:00 a.m. to 4:45 p.m. except major holidays. Admission free.

For More Information:
Fullerton Aboretum
California State University at Fullerton
Fullerton, CA 92634
(714) 773-3579

South Coast Botanic Garden
Palos Verdes

You forget you're in a garden. You're walking along, enjoying the trees and the flowers, when all of a sudden a sign identifying a bush reminds you that there's some semblance of order here. — GARDEN VISITOR

 EGUN in 1960 to hide a trash dump, South Coast Botanic Garden belies its heritage with gently rolling hills, little streams, ponds, specialty gardens, and forests of fruit trees, redwoods, palms, and pines. Over 2,000 species of plants and 200 species of birds thrive on these 87 acres.

Stepping-stones encourage visitors to walk through flower beds.

Garden Highlights

The Garden

Just inside the main entrance, you're met with a patchwork spread of color. California poppies (*Eschscholzia californica*) mix with irises, ranunculus, and lilies. Flowering plants from Australia, the Mediterranean, and South Africa provide color year round. Miniature roses grow in the center of the garden, and prize dahlias bloom from June to September. Pathways lead to the individual garden plots, while stepping-stones let you walk among the plants for a closer look.

The Shade Garden

Baskets of fuchsias—ranging from pale pink to brilliant crimson—hang from wooden slats. Pink and white impatiens, orange clivia, and soft-colored bromeliads nestle in planters throughout. Ferns and ginger also grow well in the moist, tropical atmosphere.

California poppies *(Eschscholzia californica)*.

Herb Plot

The South Bay Herb Society maintains a garden where you'll find herbs for fragrance, medicinal purposes, kitchen use, and for dyes. Fragrant herbs include rose geranium, lavender, and iris. Kitchen herbs such as dill, garlic, sage, tarragon, and oregano mingle with various types of mint. In olden days, the leaves of yarrow (*Achillea borealis*) were steeped in hot water and applied to cuts and wounds to stop the bleeding. Also useful as a dye, yarrow grows along with goldenrod and madder.

Vegetable Garden

Volunteers raise everything from artichokes to rhubarb, then donate them to a local Meals-On-Wheels charity group. Artichoke plants are a favorite with school children, who are always surprised to see the vegetable growing on bushes.

Roses

Top picks of the All-America Rose Selection cluster in a small, densely planted garden. Hybrid teas, miniatures, floribundas, and grandifloras all grow here. Look for the hybrid tea rose Peace—the All-America Rose Selection in 1946—with its yellow petals trimmed in pale pink.

Cactus and Succulent Garden

Gently mounded hillsides display plants from Africa, Mexico, South America, and the United States. The graceful palo verde (Spanish for "green stick") tree lends its name to the city of Palos Verdes. Aloes, with their brilliant red and orange spikes, bloom profusely in January. Various forms of *Opuntia* (including *Opuntia basilaris*, or beavertail cactus) flower in spring with blossoms of red, orange, magenta, and yellow.

Flowering Fruit Trees

Visit the garden in early spring to see a spectacular display of cherry, plum, apricot, and peach trees in bloom. Puffs of pink and white blossoms swirl in the breeze. Blue-flowering plants nearby include blue hibiscus.

Redwoods and Other Trees

The coast redwood (*Sequoia sempervirens*) and inland redwood (*S. gigantea*) are both displayed at South Coast Botanic Garden. The trees you see are 30 years old. Fifty species of eucalyptus and 20 species of ficus appear throughout the gardens along with ginkgo trees, Monterey pines, Japanese black pines, and the official tree of the City of Los Angeles—the red-flowering coral (*Erythrina*).

The majority of palm trees command a rise at one end of the garden. Not unlike a throne, the spot provides a regal view. Here, king and queen palms soar above date and fan palms.

Birds

South Coast Botanic Garden's specialty bird is Allen's humming-bird (*Selasphorus sasin*), a year-round resident. Look for it hovering around red-flowering bottlebrush and Mexican bush sage. Around the pond and stream you'll see great blue herons and green herons in winter and mallards, great egrets, and black-crowned night herons all year. Four to six gadwalls (*Anas strepera*), uncommon for the area, recently visited on the pond.

Red-tailed and red-shouldered hawks soar above you in fall and winter. The red-shouldered hawks nest nearby. Rock, mourning, and spotted doves are year-round residents. Look in the palm sections to spot all three.

Barn owls nest in the two major plantings of palms—look for them near Crenshaw Boulevard and near Rolling Hills Road. In winter, check out the casuarina trees (across the paved road from the weather station) for red-breasted sapsuckers (*Sphyrapicus ruber*). You may also see them in the big willow tree in the middle of the large lawn. Hooded orioles (*Icterus cucullatus*) nest in the tall palms by the weather station. Black phoebes nest under the stream bridge and can sometimes be spotted flitting from tree to tree on the lawn.

Cacti.

For more about the birds of South Coast Botanic Garden, pick up a checklist (provided by the Palos Verdes Peninsula Audubon Society) at the gift shop. The list tells you what birds you can expect to see at the garden and when.

Bird walks conducted by the Palos Verdes Peninsula Audubon Society convene the first Sunday and third Wednesday of each month at 8:00 a.m. Weekend walks usually attract about 20 birders; weekday walks about 10. The local Audubon Society meets at South Coast Botanic Garden on the last Tuesday of the month at 7:30 p.m.

Mammals, Amphibians, Insects

The stream running through the lower portion of the gardens attracts dragonflies, damselflies, frogs, birds, opposums, foxes, skunks, and rabbits. Look for the dragonfly known as the multi-colored darner, blue-green with light yellow markings down the side of its body. Small fish called gambusia, which feed on mosquito larvae, swim among the water hyacinths.

The garden is alive with butterflies, especially in mid-summer. It's one of the sites for the annual butterfly count held on the Palos Verdes Peninsula (usually in mid-July).

Cassia and acacia trees near the flowering plum and coral trees attract pure yellow sulphur butterflies. These include the cloudless or giant sulphur (*Phoebis sennae*), which feeds on wild senna. The most unusual butterfly is the sleepy orange sulphur (*Eurema nicippe*), so named because it flies more slowly than other sulphurs.

Additional butterflies you'll find breeding at the garden are the west coast lady (*Vanessa carye*), which feeds on mallows; the painted lady (*V. cardui*), which feeds on thistles; and the red admiral (*V. atalanta*). Monarch butterflies (*Danaus plexippus*) breed on the garden's milkweed plants. Anise swallowtails (*Papilio zelicaon*) and western tiger swallowtails (*P. rutulus*) feed on the garden's fennel.

Blue butterflies include the marine blue (*Leptotes marina*), which feeds on the buds and blossoms of wisteria, alfalfa, locoweed, and other legumes. The pygmy blue (*Brephidium exilis*)—the smallest species in all North American—and the Acmon blue (*Plebejus acmon*) also flutter around the gardens.

The white cabbage butterfly (*Pieris rapae*) is one of the first to emerge in spring. Common hairstreaks (*Strymon melinus*) are attracted to flowers, while mourning cloak butterflies (*Nymphalis antiopa*) feed on Chinese elms. You'll also see buckeyes (*Junonia coenia*) and half a dozen skipper species.

Spiders

In late summer or early fall, check around the northern edge of the gardens where the plants are tended less often. You may find examples of two three-inch garden spiders: the banded garden spider (*Aranea trifasciata*) and the golden garden spider (*A. aurantia*).

Tours and Activities

Docents lead garden tours every Sunday from 1:00 to 1:45 p.m., taking visitors to the garden highlights while explaining interesting aspects of the plants. Lecture programs and shows take place every Sunday at 2:00 p.m. Examples have included a world-renowned botanist lecturing on his experiences collecting and propagating succulents of the United States, Mexico, and South America. A program on spring vegetable gardening covered what to plant and when, followed by a stroll through the vegetable garden.

Location:
Five miles south of the San Diego Freeway (I-405) Crenshaw Boulevard exit.

Hours and Admission:
Open daily from 9:00 a.m. to 5:00 p.m.; closed December 25. Admission Fee.

For More Information:
South Coast Botanic Garden
26300 Crenshaw Blvd.
Palos Verdes, CA 90274
(213) 377-0468

University of California, Riverside Botanic Gardens

Riverside

> *What do I like best? I like the feeling of surprise. You don't really know what you'll see until you stumble upon it.* — GARDEN VISITOR

MEANDERING pathways take you up, down, around, and through an ever-changing variety of plants and terrain. One minute you're walking past beavertail cacti in bloom, the next you're in a forest of sequoias, mulberries, and alders.

The 39 acres contain almost 3,000 plant species. The time to visit for the most color is in April and May when the wild flowers and bearded irises bloom. Orange- and red-flowering aloes put on their show from December through March along with pink- and magenta-flowering ice plant. Roses bloom from April to December.

The most unusual trees you'll find are the Chinese parasol tree (*Firmiana simplex*) with its umbrellalike leaves, the ginkgo tree (*Ginkgo biloba*) with its fan-shaped leaves, and the golden-rain tree (*Koelreuteria bipinnata*) with its bright yellow flowers.

Arbol de barril.

Garden Highlights

Desert Garden

Aloes, cacti, yuccas, agaves, wild flowers, and ice plant nestle along the garden's northern border. Springtime is spectacular here as the beavertail cactus blooms with magenta flowers. Arbol de barril, a cousin of the ocotillo, attracts you with its enormous white flowers. Seas of brilliant ice plant (*Mesembryanthemum*) cover the hillsides, and South African daisies and toadflax (*Linaria maroccana*) line the paths. Look for bladderpod (*Isomeris arborea*), whose pods were cooked in stews or eaten right off the plant by early California natives.

Bearded iris.

Roses

Both wild and cultivated roses bloom in the northeast section of the gardens, some of them rambling, sprawling, and tumbling down the hillside. You'll find miniature, floribunda, grandiflora, and hybrid tea roses in this section.

Irises

Time your visit from March through May to see the bearded iris (*Iris germanica*) in full bloom. The garden contains 150 named irises. Look for the purple Mary McClellan, the peach-colored Lorna Lee and Sunday Chimes, and the dark ominous bloom of the Mad Hatter. According to a garden brochure, some of the purple ones smell like grape juice. I smelled them. They did! Or was it the power of suggestion?

Herb Garden

Lemon verbena (*Aloysia triphylla*), rosemary (*Rosmarinus officinalis*), lemongrass (*Cymbopogon citratus*), and numerous mints perfume the herb garden.

Alder Canyon

A pathway takes you from the pond in the northeastern section of the garden through a shady forest of California bay laurels (*Umbellularia californica*), cedar trees, sycamores (*Platanus racemosa*), and alders (*Alnus rhombifolia*).

Birds

More than 200 kinds of birds have been spotted in the garden.

The herb garden at U.C. Riverside.

Pick up a checklist at the garden gatehouse. The detailed list includes when each species might be in the gardens and what your chances are of spotting them. Commonly seen are red-shouldered and red-tailed hawks, kestrels, California quail, mourning and spotted doves, roadrunners, barn and great-horned owls, and Costa's and Anna's hummingbirds. Look for northern flickers (except in summer), black phoebes, scrub jays, and ravens. Cooper's hawks (*Accipiter cooperii*) nest in Alder Canyon.

Mammals

Animals that live at the gardens are, for the most part, nocturnal, so the chances of you seeing them are slim. Visit early in the morning or late in the afternoon for the best chance of seeing opossums, coyotes, gray foxes (*Urocyon cinereoargenteus*), and California ground squirrels. Also living in the gardens are pocket gophers, kangaroo rats, pack rats, and spotted skunks. Bobcats have been sighted.

Fish, Reptiles, Amphibians

Slender salamanders (*Batrachoseps attenuatus*), Pacific tree frogs (*Hyla regilla*), bullfrogs, western toads, and red-eared turtles frequent the pond. The water holds bluegill and brilliantly colored koi. Cattails (*Typha latifolia*) and papyrus (*Cyperus papyrus*) line the banks while Montezuma cypress (*Taxodium mucronatum*) looms above.

Rose garden.

Snakes and lizards also inhabit the gardens, but are rarely seen. Snakes include the California king, gopher (*Pituophis catenifer*), red diamond rattlesnake, red racer, and rosy boa. Lizards include alligator, western fence (*Sceloporus occidentalis*), western skink, and western whiptail.

Tours

To get as much as possible out of a short period of time, purchase a copy of "The Outdoor Classroom" at the main entrance. It takes you on a 45-minute loop around the gardens and, at each numbered stop, fills you in on what you're seeing. Call to arrange for group tours ahead of time. Children under 16 must be accompanied by an adult.

Location:

From the University Avenue exit of either US 60 or US 215, follow the signs to the Botanic Gardens on the University of California, Riverside campus.

Hours and Admission:

Open daily from 8:00 a.m. to 5:00 p.m.; closed January 1, July 4, Thanksgiving, and December 25. Admission free.

For More Information:

University of California, Riverside
Botanic Gardens
Riverside, CA 92521
(714) 787-4650

Rancho Santa Ana Botanic Garden

Claremont

The world's favorite season is the spring. All things seem possible in May. – EDWIN WAY TEALE

 ANCHO Santa Ana Botanic Garden is so big—85 acres—that it's easy to get lost, especially in the northern reaches where trails tend to wind around and over themselves. Getting lost here, however, is fun, since you tend to bump into plants and flowers you wouldn't have found otherwise.

The garden features all California natives, arranged according to their natural distribution throughout the state. The diversity ranges from a riparian trail and streamside garden to a desert garden and a planting of conifers. The garden is best visited in spring, from early February—when there may still be snow on Mount Baldy looming in the background—through June.

Wild flowers grow profusely in small plantings scattered throughout the garden. Brodiaeas, farewell-to-spring (*Clarkia*), the petite yellow flowers of meadowfoam, and, of course, California poppies bloom everywhere you turn. The best time to see them is mid-March through the end of May.

Garden walkway.

Garden Highlights

Desert Garden
Mid-April through late May is the ideal time to visit the Desert Garden to see the yellow, orange, pink, and magenta colors of beavertail cactus,

prickly pear, and desert willow in bloom. This garden contains just about every cactus species in California, along with desert shrubs and succulents.

Coastal Garden

The plants here represent the 845 miles of California shoreline. They range from the thick-leaved, purple-magenta flowered sea fig (*Carpobrotus aequilaterus*) to dune manzanita (*Arctostaphylos pumila*).

Woodland and Riparian Trails

Oak and walnut trees provide welcome shade on hot, sunny days. Look for Cooper's hawks in the trees and rufous-sided towhees scrabbling about in the understory. Lined with deciduous trees, the Riparian Trail particularly attracts the birds. A great egret can often be seen near one of the ponds.

Manzanita Display Area

Visit the garden from mid-December through February to see an impressive display of manzanita (*Arctostaphylos*) in full bloom. The plants range from small, low-growing specimens to large plants that look more like trees.

Ceanothus Collection

Known as California lilacs, blue-flowering ceanothus plants are covered with flowers (and bees!) from early March to late April.

Location:
North of Foothill and east of Indian Hill boulevards on North College Avenue.

Hours and Admission:
Open daily from 8:00 a.m. to 5:00 p.m.; closed January 1, July 4, Thanksgiving, and December 25. Admission free.

For More Information:
Rancho Santa Ana Botanic Garden
1500 North College Avenue
Claremont, CA 91711-3101
(714) 625-8767

Mildred E. Mathias
Botanical Gardens
Los Angeles

*Great things are done when men and
    mountains meet;
This is not done by jostling in the street.*
                                    — WILLIAM BLAKE

OUR thousand species of plants, representing 225 families, cover eight acres of Westwood hillside. They grow along shady creeks, bask in sunny open beds, and climb up gentle slopes.

Two entrances lead into the gardens: one at the top of the canyon, the other at the bottom. Entering from the top (off Tiverton Avenue near UCLA Medical Center), you have an eye-level view of the treetops, including California fan palms (*Washingtonia filifera*) and an enormous Torrey pine (*Pinus torreyana*). Enter from the bottom (at LeConte and Hilgard), and you're greeted with cypress trees and dawn redwoods (*Metasequoia glyptostroboides*).

Rose gums (*Eucalyptus grandis*) in the Australian section rise 200 feet above you, while pathways lined with liriope and mondo grass attract your gaze downward. Especially noted for its large collection of tropical plants, the garden includes torch ginger, bamboo, banana trees, ferns, clivia, and orchids.

Paths take you across ponds and little streams by footbridge, past lily

Orange clivia.

beds (with lilies from every continent), Australian and Central and South American plants, rhododendrons, native California species, palms, and conifers. All in all, the garden presents a truly eclectic mix of geographic regions and plant types.

Location:
Adjoining Mira Hershey Hall at the southwest corner of Westwood's University of California, Los Angeles campus.

Hours and Admission:
Open daily from 8:00 a.m. except university holidays, closing weekdays at 5:00 and weekends at 4:30 p.m. Admission free.

For More Information:
Mildred E. Mathias Botanical Gardens
University of California, Los Angeles
Los Angeles, CA 90024
(213) 825-4321 or 826-3620

Virginia Robinson Gardens

Beverly Hills

*He that plants trees loves others besides
himself.* — ENGLISH PROVERB

 HERE was just one elderberry bush on the property when Virginia Robinson and her husband Harry (of J.W. Robinson's department store fame) built their Beverly Hills home in 1911. The elderberry bush is gone now, but in its place are 6.2 acres of terraced plantings and patio gardens with azaleas, roses, cycads, camellias, banana trees, and palms.

A two-acre palm grove contains one of the finest stands of

Azaleas.

king palms in the United States. Footpaths take you past towering banana trees, fishtail palms, and the banyan-like roots of a Port Jackson fig. The Los Angeles County Department of Arboreta and Botanic Gardens operates an experimental garden at the bottom of the palm grove and is currently working with ginger plants.

On the other side of the estate—divided by a lawn, swimming pool, and pool house—interlocking pathways take you beside white, pink, and deep red azaleas and rhododendrons. Two stone lions stare regally down the slope where hibiscus, camellia, clivia, and fruit trees crowd the pathways.

A small rose garden blossoms in summer next to the tennis court. Perennials bloom continually around the lawn and pool area. Look for the orange, red, and pink Joseph's Coat rose planted on the eastern side of the lawn.

Tours

The only way to visit the garden is to reserve a spot on a one-hour tour. A knowledgeable guide will tell you the history of the estate, point out the more unusual plants, and take you to the very best the gardens have to offer. April and May are the prettiest times to visit, but the gardens are lovely year round.

Location:
In Beverly Hills.

Hours and Admission:
Open only for tours Tuesday through Friday at 10:00 a.m. and 1:00 p.m. Admission fee.

For More Information:
Robinson Garden Tours
Los Angeles County Department
of Arboreta and Botanic Gardens
301 N. Baldwin Ave.
Arcadia, CA 91006
(310) 466-8251

Huntington Botanical Gardens
San Marino

Half our life is spent trying to find something to do with the time we have rushed through life trying to save. — WILL ROGERS

 IKE a French impressionist painting, the broad lawns, arbors, and pathways at Huntington Botanical Gardens invoke a feeling of tranquility, as if time has slowed just for the afternoon. Combine this feeling of serenity with the breathtaking beauty of the surroundings, and you come close to heaven. The gardens are enormous—130 acres—with 14,000 varieties of trees and plants. So take your time and savor the afternoon as you slowly explore this fantastic garden.

Garden Highlights

Azalea-Camellia Garden

This is the largest public collection of camellias and azaleas in the world—brilliant from late winter to early spring when the 175 varieties of azaleas and 2,000 camellia cultivars bloom in shades from creamy white to the deepest red. Photographers invariably gravitate to this section, drawn by the vivid colors.

Shakespeare Garden

A small pocket of a garden brims with plants popular during Shakespeare's time. "There's rosemary, that's for remembrance; pray, love,

Palm Garden.

remember: and there is pansies, that's for thoughts"—not to mention medieval European roses, daffodils, carnations, columbines, and poppies. Butterflies attracted to the garden include painted ladies (*Vanessa cardui*), mourning cloaks (*Nymphalis antiopa*), and red admirals (*Vanessa atalanta*). If you're lucky, you may spot California's state butterfly, the California dogface (*Zerene eurydice*), also known as the "flying pansy." With markings on each wing resembling a dog's face looking away from the butterfly's body, these yellow, orange, and black insects are usually seen in June and July.

Rose Garden

More than 1,200 varieties trace a thousand years of rose history. Examples range from hybrids, teas, and climbers to Chinese roses.

Japanese Garden

A small pond surrounded with yellow iris, pine, bamboo, magnolia, wisteria, and graceful willows rests in a five-acre canyon. A red-orange moon bridge completes a circle with its reflection in the pond. A zigzag bridge (designed to foil demons, who travel only in straight lines) takes you to the Zen Garden created from raked gravel and carefully selected rocks and plants.

Near the pond in midsummer you may find Baird's swallowtail butterfly (*Papilio bairdii*); its lighter-colored relative, the pale tiger swallowtail (*Pterourus eurymdeon*); and the handsome western tiger swallowtail (*P. rutulus*).

Moon bridge.

Desert Garden

It may sound strange to use the word lush in describing a desert garden, but here it's an accurate description. This is the largest outdoor collection in the world. Twelve acres of ocotillos, yuccas, floss silk trees, puyas, mammillaria, opuntias, and euphorbias sprawl, ramble, tower, flower, and climb.

Birds

Anna's hummingbirds (*Calypte anna*) visit the ocotillos' red blooms in early spring. You may also see black-chinned (*Archilochus alexandri*) and Costa's hummingbirds (*Calypte costae*) in the Desert Garden. Purple finches, Cassin's finches, and house finches are fond of the area too. You'll often see them perched atop a cactus, singing loudly.

The garden's most unusual bird is the red-whiskered bulbul (*Pycnonotus jocosus*). The buff, brown, and beige bird has a black crest and a distinctive bright red patch behind the ear and under the tail. The Palm Garden attracts black and orange hooded orioles (*Icterus cucullatus*). Bright yellow and orange western tanagers (*Piranga ludoviciana*) sometimes flit about in the larger trees bordering the lawns.

Tours

Tours of the garden begin Tuesday through Friday at 1:00 p.m.

Location:
Twelve miles northeast of downtown Los Angeles on Oxford Road in San Marino.

Hours and Admission:
Open Tuesday through Sunday from 1:00 to 4:30 p.m.; closed holidays. Reservations required for Sunday. Admission free, but a $5 donation per person suggested.

For More Information:
Huntington Library, Art Collections and Botanical Gardens
1151 Oxford Road
San Marino, CA 91108
(818) 405-2100, 405-2141, or 405-2275

Los Angeles State and County Arboretum

Arcadia

Pride sits you well, so strut, colossal bird.
— MARIANNE MOORE

OZENS of peafowl, often with their tail feathers in full display, roam the arboretum's 127 acres like royalty. Although the peafowl might be the most obvious—and noisiest—attraction, there's a lot to explore: tropical greenhouses, an ornate Victorian home, an old adobe, a railroad depot, ponds, water gardens, and more. The arboretum welcomes visitors under the age of 18 only when accompanied by an adult.

Garden Highlights

Tropical Greenhouse

Bromeliads, orchids, and ferns create a steamy tropical atmosphere enhanced by little streams, pools, and waterfalls. The rain forest setting contains maidenhair and pale green bird's nest ferns, colorful crotons, and the heart-shaped red and pink flowers of anthuriums. The greenhouse also features one of the largest displays of cattleya and cymbidium orchids in the United States.

Peacock.

Meadowbrook

Designed as a showcase for landscape plants, this area combines birches and daffodils, magnolia trees, and a large perennial garden. Grassy patches separate a number of small ponds; Japanese maples, irises, and purple-blooming jacaranda trees surround one filled with water lilies and koi. Canada, Chinese, and greylag geese live here year round. Great blue herons sometimes wait motionless next to the koi pond, looking for unwary fish to swim within beak's range.

Aquatic Garden

Water hyacinths and water lilies grow in a waterfall-fed pond atop Tallac Knoll. Tree ferns, pines, irises, and sword ferns add color and a tropical look to the scene.

Australian and African Sections

Over 300 species of eucalyptus, yellow-flowering acacia, and 24 species of bottlebrush (*Callistemon*) fill the Australian section with plants well-suited to Southern California's mild climate. The African Section's hundreds of aloes bloom in late winter in colors of orange, red, and yellow.

Historical Sites

If the beautifully maintained Victorian Queen Anne Cottage seems familiar, you may recall seeing it on the television series "Fantasy Island," where Tattoo announced "Da plane! Da plane!" on a weekly basis. Built in 1885 by Elias J. "Lucky" Baldwin, the house nestles among tall (up to 125 feet high) fan palms (*Washingtonia robusta*) at the edge of Lasca Lagoon.

Lasca Lagoon—one of the few natural freshwater lakes in Southern California— served as the backdrop where Katharine Hepburn and Humphrey Bogart fought leeches and the Germans in *The African Queen*. Stands of papyrus surround the lake along with 27 varieties of coral trees (*Erythrina*), the official tree of the City of Los Angeles.

Lasca Lagoon.

An 1879 Victorian coach barn (once used to house Baldwin's carriages), a Mexican adobe, a Native American wickiup, and a restored Santa Fe Railroad depot are also worth a look.

Butterflies

You may see the western black swallowtail (*Papilio bairdii*) and the short-tailed black swallowtail (*P. indra*) in the wetter areas of the arboretum from late spring into summer. Both gather nectar from mint, so look for them around the Herb Garden. In June, July, and August you may also find the two-tailed tiger swallowtail (*Pterourus multicaudatus*), the largest tiger swallowtail in the West. Look for its lighter-colored cousin, the pale tiger swallowtail (*P. eurymedon*), from May to July.

Sara orange-tips (*Anthocharis sara*), creamy white butterflies with bright orange wing tips, flutter around the gardens from February into July. The pale orange snout butterfly (*Libytheana bachmanii*) tends toward the wooded sections of the arboretum from September through November.

Like their cousins, the painted ladies (*Vanessa cardui*), American painted ladies (*V. virginiensis*) flock to more open, sunnier areas. You'll find both of them from June to September.

The big orange slow-flying monarch butterflies (*Danaus plexippus*) are easy to spot. Check the Shasta daisies for mourning cloaks (*Nymphalis antiopa*). Lorquin's admirals (*Basilarchia lorquini*) frequent the waterfall and pond areas from April to September.

Birds

At Lasca Lagoon, you'll see double-crested cormorants (*Phalacrocorax auritus*) and perhaps a black-crowned night heron perched in the surrounding trees. The lake also attracts mallards and large numbers of ring-necked ducks. Look for an occasional wigeon or pintail among the ring-necks.

Bird walks begin at 8:00 a.m. the first Sunday of the month. Perhaps you'll see the red-whiskered bulbul or the small flock of Amazon parrots that sometimes goes screeching through the gardens.

Tours

The arboretum offers tram tours on weekdays between 12:15 and 3:00 p.m. and on weekends between 10:30 a.m. and 4:00 p.m., waiving the $1.50 fee every third Tuesday of each month.

Location:

In Arcadia, 15 miles northeast of downtown Los Angeles.

Hours and Admission:

Open daily from 9:00 a.m. to 5.00 p.m.; closed December 25. Begonia greenhouse open weekdays from 10:00 a.m. to 4:30 p.m. Tropical greenhouse open daily from 9:00 a.m. to 4:30 p.m. Admission fee.

For More Information:

Los Angeles State and County Arboretum
301 N. Baldwin Avenue
Arcadia, CA 91006-2697
(818) 821-3222

Descanso Gardens

La Cañada-Flintridge

There ought to be moments of tranquility in great works. — VOLTAIRE

 WALK through Descanso Gardens can be tranquil on cool, misty mornings. Sunlight filters through the branches of California oaks to light dewdrops glittering on pearly white camellia blossoms. A walk through Descanso Gardens can also be a riot of color as bright red tulips and sunny yellow daffodils burst forth in spring or All-American roses vie for attention in summer. Whichever appeals to you—cool shade under the oaks or bright sun in the rose garden—you'll find it at Descanso Gardens.

Garden Highlights

Flowers

Famous for its camellias, Descanso Gardens offers 600 varieties (*japonica, reticulata,* and *sasanqua*) ranging from the purest white to the deepest red. Some of the 100,000 bushes stand more than ten feet tall. In bloom from October through March, they flourish in the mottled shade under 30 acres of California oaks (*Quercus agrifolia*).

The annual spring flower show begins in March with the

largest flowering collection of tulips on the West Coast—20,000 bulbs in full bloom. Narcissus, ixia, and Dutch iris add to the colorful display along with 10,000 daffodils.

Yellow tulips.

Summer is the best time to visit Descanso's five-acre Rose Garden, which features every All-American Rose Selection (AARS) winner since 1940 (in bloom from May to December). An Old-Fashioned Rose Garden displays one of each variety of old garden rose cultivated since 1200 B.C. The oldest? Look for the red Gallica, originally grown by the Persians. Because the historical roses appear in chronological order, you can easily see how our modern hybrid tea roses developed. The Old-Fashioned Garden peaks in May and early June.

Of special interest is a large grove of lilacs, rarely found in California. For those of us who grew up in the South or on the East Coast, a whiff of these blossoms in April brings back fond memories.

Not to be outdone by the colors of tulips, daffodils, and camellias in the spring, more than 200 varieties of azaleas and rhododendrons bloom throughout the gardens in early March and April.

Birds

Flowers aren't the only reason to visit Descanso Gardens. In 1991, the garden combined two ponds to create a 1.5-acre lake that has rapidly become popular with birds and birders. Two observation stations provide excellent vantage points for ob-

Small waterfall at Descanso Gardens.

serving waterfowl like wood ducks and mallards. Large numbers of ring-necked ducks enjoy the lake, as do belted kingfishers, green herons, and great blue herons. In summer you may be lucky enough to see the sleek black feathers of a phainopepla snatching insects out of the air.

Oak trees throughout the gardens are excellent places to look for resident woodpeckers—acorn, Nuttall's, downy, and the common flicker. Red-shouldered hawks nest in February (listen for their distinctive call). Cooper's hawks and great horned owls have also been spotted. Gangs of cedar waxwings rove through the gardens in winter like masked bandits, feeding on pyracantha, toyon, and other berries. Meet at the Gatehouse for bird walks held every second and fourth Sunday of the month at 8:00 a.m.

Tours

For a small fee, the garden offers guided jeep tram tours Tuesday through Friday from 1:00 p.m. to 3:00 p.m. and weekends and holidays from 11:00 a.m. to 3:00 p.m.

After your meanderings through the garden, stop by the Japanese Tea House (open between 11:00 a.m. and 4:00 p.m. Tuesday through Sunday). It's the perfect place to rest, drink tea, and eat cookies. A small stream splashes in the background as you relax and enjoy the lush greenery of a formal Japanese garden. For works of art other than those provided by nature, drop by Hospitality House in the upper reaches of the gardens to see monthly shows by artists of their work.

Location:
Near the interchange of Interstate 210 and the Glendale Freeway (2).

Hours and Admission:
Open daily from 9:00 a.m. to 4:30 p.m.; closed December 25. Admission fee, but free the third Tuesday of each month.

For More Information:
Descanso Gardens
1418 Descanso Drive
La Cañada-Flintridge, CA 91011
(818) 790-5414

Antelope Valley California Poppy Reserve

Lancaster

To see a World in a Grain of Sand,
And a Heaven in a Wild Flower,
Hold Infinity in the palm of your hand,
And Eternity in an hour. — WILLIAM BLAKE

 FTER a wet winter in Southern California, there are few sites more spectacular than the rolling hills around Lancaster covered with the fiery golden glow of millions of California poppies (*Eschscholzia californica*). At the height of the season, you can see the orange-covered hills from nine miles away.

Visit in April, when the poppies and purplish blue miniature lupines (*Lupinus bicolor*) bloom in tandem. Bird residents include meadowlarks and horned larks (quite fearless as they skitter ahead of you on the sidewalks around the Interpretive Center).

California poppies.

Look for other flowers blooming in the area like shocking pink owl's clover (*Orthocarpus purpuracens*), bright yellow desert dandelion (*Malacothrix glabrata*), and reddish lavender filaree (*Erodium cicuurtarum*). Throughout the month of April you can call the Lancaster Chamber of Commerce, (805) 948-4518, for the best blooming times and locations.

Location:
Approximately 13 miles west of the Antelope Valley Freeway (14) on Lancaster Road, an extension of Avenue I.

Hours and Admission:
Open to view year round. Interpretive Center open during wildflower season weekdays from 10:00 a.m. to 3:00 p.m., weekends from 9:00 a.m. to 4:00 p.m. Parking fee at the Interpretive Center, or simply stop your car and park on the side of the road.

For More Information:
Antelope Valley California Poppy Reserve
California Department of Parks and Recreation
15101 W. Lancaster Road
Lancaster, CA 93536
(805) 942-0662

Fields of ranunculi in Carlsbad.

Flower Fields
Carlsbad

MORE than 80 acres of ranunculi come into full bloom around mid-March behind Pea Soup Andersen's restaurant in Carlsbad. Drivers can easily spot the rainbow strips of flowers from the freeway. You're welcome to stop, admire the scene, and even walk through the fields. You just can't pick the flowers! Owned by Frazee Flowers, the commercial fields flank the east side of the San Diego Freeway opposite South Carlsbad State Beach Park. Look for the huge Dutch windmill.

Mission San Luis Rey
Oceanside

THE first pepper tree planted in California (1830) still grows at Mission San Luis Rey. It shades the friary garden next to the mission. Otherwise fairly unremarkable, the gardens contain aloe, oleander, and ice plant. You'll find the mission along State Route 76 at 4050 Mission Avenue. For more information, call (619) 757-3651.

Mission San Juan Capistrano

San Juan Capistrano

LANTANA, bird of paradise, pepper trees, poinsettias, *Cotoneaster rosaceae*, cape honeysuckle, and lots of bougainvillea landscape the grounds of this lovely mission. The small Paul Arbiso Rose Garden delights rose lovers with well-tended plants. In the Baja Garden you'll see barrel cactus, aloe, agave, and prickly pear. Open daily from 8:30 a.m. to 5:00 p.m. October 1 to May 14; 8:30 a.m. to 7:00 p.m. May 15 to September 30. Modest admission fee. For more information, contact Mission San Juan Capistrano, Ortega Highway and Camino Capistrano, San Juan Capistrano, CA 92675. Or call (714) 493-1855.

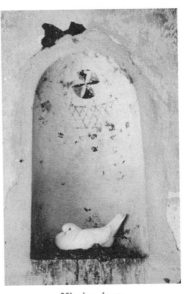

Mission dove.

Rancho Los Alamitos Historic Site

Long Beach

UNTIL 1953, this was a working cattle operation with an old adobe, ranch house, barn, and stables. The original adobe (built in 1806) still stands. Oleanders, desert plants, roses, and herbs landscape four acres of grounds. Open Wednesday through Sunday from 1:00 to 5:00 p.m. Admission free. For more information, contact Rancho Los Alamitos Historic Site, 6400 Bixby Hill Road, Long Beach, CA 90815. Or call (310) 431-3541.

Rancho Los Cerritos Historic Site

Long Beach

VISIT in spring and summer when a variety of colorful flowers bloom. Some of the trees around the adobe (built in 1837) are over 100 years old. For more information, contact Rancho Los Cerritos Historic Site, 4600 Virginia Road, Long Beach, CA 90807. Or call (310) 424-9423.

Rose Hills Memorial Park

Whittier

THE 3.5-acre Pageant of Roses Garden highlights Rose Hills Memorial Park. More than 7,000 bushes show off 750 varieties of roses. Ponds mirror arched bridges in a Japanese garden, and deer often roam the grounds. Open daily from 8:00 a.m. to 5:00 p.m. Admission free. For more information, contact Rose Hills Memorial Park, 3900 S. Workman Mill Road, Whittier, CA 90601. Or call (213) 699-0921.

Echo Park Lotus Pond

Los Angeles

SHOCKINGLY lovely lotus blossoms (*Nelumbo nucifera*) bloom at the northern end of Echo Park's lake from mid-June through

July. Always a draw for photographers, the enormous blossoms raise their heads above the water just offshore. You'll find the pond at the intersection of Glendale Boulevard and Park Avenue.

Lotus blossom in Echo Park.

Exposition Park Rose Garden
Los Angeles

AMERICA'S largest sunken rose garden covers seven acres with 16,000 bushes. The flowers range from the pink Queen Elizabeth to the fragrant yellow Lemon Spice to the deep red Olympia. Visit the garden—on Exposition Boulevard between Figueroa and Vermont streets—in April and May when the roses are at their peak. For more information, contact the City of Los Angeles, Department of Parks, City Hall East, Room 1350, 200 N. Main Street, Los Angeles, CA 90012. Or call (213) 748-4772 to reach the Rose Garden; (213) 485-5515 to reach the Department of Parks.

James Irvine Garden
Los Angeles

THIS is one of those small hidden gardens that not many people know about—and you hope they never do. So let's keep this our little secret. Just getting into the garden makes you feel like you're in on something. You enter the Japanese-American Cultural and Community Center in Little Tokyo and take the elevator to the basement. A short hallway leads to the garden where azaleas bloom in colors of pink, red, and white each spring. A winding stream with tiny waterfalls splashes over little rocks and around the plants. The garden lies a half block south of 2nd Street on San Pedro Street. Open daily from 9:00 a.m. to 5:00 p.m., except holidays. Admission free. For more information, contact the Japanese American Cultural and Community Center, 244 S. San Pedro Street, Los Angeles, CA 90012. Or call (213) 628-2725.

James Irvine Garden.

New Otani Hotel Japanese Garden

Los Angeles

AS WITH the James Irvine Garden, few people know about the garden at the top of the New Otani Hotel. Take the elevator to the roof where a small stream bordered by cattails, a little pond, waterfalls, and spring-blooming azaleas contrast with the view of skyscrapers and bustle of the city below. For more information, contact the New Otani Hotel, 120 S. Los Angeles Street, Los Angeles, CA 90012. Or call (213) 620-1200.

Kaizuka Meditation Garden

Culver City

DESIGNERS and workmen planned and constructed this small garden in Japan, then dismantled it and sent it to the Culver City Library for assembly. The garden—at 4975 Overland Avenue in Culver City—includes a stone bridge and koi pond. For more information, contact the Culver City Department of Parks and Recreation, 4117 Overland Boulevard, Culver City, CA 90230. Or call (213) 837-5211.

UCLA Hannah Carter Japanese Garden

Los Angeles

A GARDEN so small and popular that reservations must be made at least 30 days in advance, California's most authentic Japanese garden features 1.5 acres of azaleas, bromeliads, live oaks, and ferns. Bridges, shrine, teahouse, and main gate were all built in Japan, shipped to California, and reassembled on site. The grounds also include a small Hawaiian garden and koi pond. Admission free. For more information, contact the UCLA Visitors Center, Dodd Hall, Room 100, 405 Hilgard Avenue, Los Angeles, CA 90024. Or call (213) 825-4574 or 206-8147.

Beverly Hills Cactus Garden
Beverly Hills

BLOCK-LONG sections define Beverly Gardens Park, a narrow strip of Beverly Hills that runs along Santa Monica Boulevard between Wilshire and Doheny boulevards. Some sections are more spectacular and interesting than others. The best of the bunch is the Beverly Hills Cactus Garden. Located on the north side of Santa Monica Boulevard between Bedford and Camden drives, the selection of cacti and succulents ranges from beavertail cacti to agaves, aloes, and dracaenas.

Chances are slim, but you may find yucca moths (*Tegeticula maculata*) fluttering around the *Yucca whipplei* plants at dusk. The yucca and its moth make the perfect example of a symbiotic relationship: The only food the moth larvae eat is from the yucca plant; the only insect able to pollinate the yucca plant is this particular moth.

Friendship Garden
Glendale

ELJIRO NUNOKAWA, who designed Descanso Gardens in La Cañada-Flintridge, also designed this Japanese garden in Brand Park. The Friendship Garden—at 1601 West Mountain in Glendale—contains a pond, stone lanterns, and a teahouse called Sho-Shei-An, which means "Teahouse of the Whispering Pines." Open daily by appointment only. Admission free. For more information, contact Parks and Recreation Division, 613 E. Broadway, Room 120, Glendale, CA 91201. Or call (213) 956-2000.

Donald C. Tillman Japanese Garden

Van Nuys

A 6.5-ACRE Japanese garden dresses up the grounds of a water treatment facility with small lakes surrounded by bamboo, azaleas, coast redwoods, magnolia trees, alders, and willows. The garden attracts great and snowy egrets and, in winter, a variety of waterfowl. Zigzag bridges, lanterns, bonsai trees, and well-tended lawns create a calm and quiet atmosphere.

Conducted tours (free) provide the only way to see the garden. Lasting just over an hour, they depart Tuesday, Thursday, and Saturday at 9:00 and 10:15 a.m. Children under 12 not admitted. For more information, contact the Donald C. Tillman Water Reclamation Plant and Japanese Garden, 6100 Woodley Avenue, Van Nuys, CA 91406. For reservations, call (818) 989-8166.

Orcutt Ranch Horticulture Center

Canoga Park

ORIGINALLY the country home of William and Mary Orcutt, Orcutt Ranch Horticulture Center consists of a small rose garden, tropical plants, ancient oaks, and citrus groves surrounding a Spanish-style ranch house built in 1920. Tours of the house take place between 2:00 and 5:00 p.m. on the last Sunday of each month (except July or August). The grounds are open daily (except holidays) between 6:00 a.m. and 5:00 p.m. Admission free. For more information, contact the Orcutt Ranch Horticulture Center, 23600 Roscoe Boulevard, Canoga Park, CA 91304. Or call (818) 883-6641.

Abbey Garden Cactus and Succulent Nursery, *Carpinteria*

Flower Fields, *Lompoc*

Hearst Castle, *San Simeon*

La Purísima Mission, *Lompoc*

Montaña de Oro State Park, *Los Osos*

University of California, Santa Cruz Arboretum, *Santa Cruz*

Abbey Garden Cactus and Succulent Nursery

Carpinteria

Let us be very strange and well-bred....
— WILLIAM CONGREVE

MATEURS and aficionados both will be astounded by this collection of cacti and succulents—over 2,000 varieties from more than 20 countries.

Examples range from dangerous to noble to bizarre to comical. Beware the sinister *Euphorbia virosa*; its markings may be handsome, but the sap is poisonous. *Mammilaria huitzilopochtli* has a name as formidable as its namesake, the Aztec god of war. Touch the white frosted leaves of *Haworthia pygmaea*—don't they feel like a cat's tongue? And whoever first called *Pelargonium gibbosum* the "chicken knees" plant described it well—take a look at those knobby, jointed stems.

Flowering cacti neatly laid out at Abbey Garden.

Location:
On Carpinteria Avenue in Carpinteria.

Hours and Admission:
Open Tuesday through Sunday from 9:00 a.m. to 5:00 p.m. Admission free.

For More Information:
Abbey Garden Cactus and Succulent Nursery
4620 Carpinteria Avenue
Carpinteria, CA 93013
(805) 684-5112

Santa Barbara Botanic Garden
Santa Barbara

One of the most peaceful experiences at the garden is a stroll along the creek amidst the golden leaves of the black cottonwood and bigleaf maple. — GARDEN BROCHURE

 PRING AND FALL are the most dramatic times to visit Santa Barbara Botanic Garden. In spring, California poppies bloom in the Meadow Section; the big pink trumpet-shaped flowers of desert-willow burst forth in the Desert Section; and stream orchids—with exotic reddish brown flowers—bloom in the Arroyo Section.

In fall, bright crimson berries appear on toyon bushes along the Pritchett Trail and on madrone trees in the Redwood Section. The Canyon Section's deciduous trees turn spectacular shades of gold and orange.

But, come to think of it, summer's pretty special here, too, with bright red California fuchsia blossoms in the Meadow Section, yucca spires rising tall and bold in the Desert Section, and bright yellow and white matilija poppies blooming in the Manzanita Section. Butterflies are more plentiful in the summer, too.

It's obvious. *Any* time you visit Santa Barbara Botanic Garden, you'll find something to see, examine, and wonder at. Five miles of easy-walking trails wind through 65 acres at a leisurely pace. Each of the ten sections features a unique selection of native California plants, trees, and flowers.

Garden Highlights

Meadow Section

Ideally visited in spring and summer, the Meadow Section's wide expanse encourages you to look far and wide, but the plant life you see brings you back to earth, inviting you to move in close to explore the intricacies of grasses and flowers.

California poppies (*Eschscholzia californica*) steal the scene in spring. But you'll also see the blue-violet flowers of blue-eyed grass (*Sisyrinchium bellum*), bright yellow California goldenrod (*Solidago californica*), and the brilliant scarlet flowers of California fuchsia (*Zauschneria californica*). The show lasts from spring into summer.

Look for pale yellow common sulphur butterflies (*Colias philodice*) and gold-colored orange sulphurs (*C. eurytheme*) throughout the summer. Both feed on the nectar of California goldenrod. You'll probably see painted ladies (*Vanessa cardui*) and American painted ladies (*V. virginiensis*) from mid-summer through September. The meadow's foothill penstemon (*Penstemon heterophyllus*) also attracts the large and exotic western black swallowtail (*Papilio bairdii*).

On the west side of the meadow, the Sellar and Bessie Bullard brook and pool offers a cool, shady place to explore. Under coast live oaks grow cattails, scarlet monkey-flowers (*Mimulus cardinalis*), bright yellow common monkey-flowers (M. guttatus), and California rose-mallow (*Hibiscus californicus*). Ferns and other shade-loving plants add to the lush tropical atmosphere. Monarch butterflies (*Danaus plexippus*) feed on California rose-mallow, and western tiger swallowtails flock to the moist, shady spots.

Desert Section

This area blooms spectacularly in spring with plants from California's desert areas. With its yellow flowers, coast prickly pear (*Opuntia oricola*) competes with goldfields (*Lasthenia*). Evening primroses (*Oenothera deltoides*) bloom at night to attract moth pollinators. Chuparosa (*Justicia californica*) flowers serve as beacons to hummingbirds, so you may see both Anna's and Costa's varieties hovering around the tubular red blossoms.

Yucca blooms on the Campbell Trail.

Campbell Trail

Beginning near the palms in the Desert Section, the Campbell Trail leads down to the canyon floor and across Mission Creek. Live-forevers (*Dudleya*) and a variety of monkey-flowers grow along the way—especially colorful in spring. *Yucca whipplei* sends its spire of flowers high above the ground from April through July. Expect rufous-sided towhees, California quail, and scrub jays in this section.

Pritchett Trail

Walk the Pritchett Trail in winter to appreciate the cool, clear air and bright red berries of toyon (*Heteromeles arbutifolia*) in full color. (Also known as Christmas berry, this hollylike plant, which grows in profusion above the Hollywood hills, is what gave the community its name.) Big-pod ceanothus (*Ceanothus megacarpus*) will also be in bloom—its white flowers dusting the Santa Ynez Mountains like snow. Cedar waxwings and hermit thrushes feed on the toyon berries. Look also for acorn and Nuttall's woodpeckers and white-breasted nuthatches.

Redwood Section

The Redwood Section promises a cool place to walk in summer and a colorful spot in autumn. Coast redwoods (*Sequoia sempervirens*) join tanbark oaks (*Lithocarpus densiflora*), hazelnut trees (*Corylus cornuta*), bigleaf maples (*Acer macrophyllum*), and madrones (*Arbutus menziesii*). In the fall, look for rufoussided towhees eating the madrone berries.

Woodland Trail

Visit from February through April to see the Woodland Trail at its most colorful. As you travel through this forest of coast live oak (*Quercus agrifolia*), you'll see lemonade berry (*Rhus integrifolia*) in bloom from February through April, redberry (*Rhamnus crocea*) in bloom in March and April, and the red flowers of hummingbird sage (*Salvia spathacea*) from March to May.

Arroyo Section

Just south of the Garden Shop, the Arroyo Section contains an impressive selection of coast redwoods, aromatic incense cedars (*Calocedrus decurrens*), Port Orford cedar (*Chamaecyparis lawsoniana*), and a giant sequoia (*Sequoiadendron giganteum*). Ferns, native irises, and stream orchids (*Epipactis gigantea*) nestle below the towering trees.

Manzanita Section

More than 30 species of manzanita grow west of the Arroyo Section. The low-growing, gnarly-branched plants bear smooth red- and cinnamon-colored bark. Visit the north end of the Manzanita Section in May and June to see a massive planting of matilija poppies (*Romneya*) in full bloom. Nicknamed "eggs over easy" or the "fried egg plant," these bushes present flowers with big yellow centers and crinkly white petals—a dramatic contrast against a deep blue sky. Nearby, a planting of pinkish lavender farewell-to-spring (*Clarkia*) blooms in April, May, and June.

Island Section

As you walk west from the Manzanita Section, you begin to wander through plants from Baja California and the Channel

Islands. Ironwood from Santa Cruz and Santa Catalina islands appears along with Santa Cruz Island buckwheat (*Eriogonum arborescens*) and island tree mallow (*Lavatera assurgentiflora*).

Canyon Section

The trail through the Canyon Section adjoins Mission Creek, lined with white alders (*Alnus rhombifolia*), aromatic California bay trees (*Umbellularia californica*), bigleaf maples, and black cottonwoods.

Porter Trail and Ceanothus Section

Often neglected by garden visitors, the Porter Trail and Ceanothus Section (across Mission Canyon Road) presents striking views of the Santa Ynez Mountains, the garden below, and islands off the California coast. Various examples of cypress trees include the Monterey cypress (*Cupressus macrocarpa*), tecate cypress (*C. forbesii*), and Macnab cypress (*C. macnabiana*). March through May you can see the twisted and gnarled plants of giant coreopsis (*Coreopsis gigantea*) in full, golden bloom along with the lilac or rose-purple flowers of notable penstemon (*Penstemon spectabilis*).

Tours

Garden tours begin Thursday and Saturday at 10:30 a.m. and Sunday at 10:30 a.m. and 2:00 p.m.

Location:
On Mission Canyon Road in Santa Barbara.

Hours and Admission:
Open daily from 8:00 a.m. to dusk. Garden Shop open from 10:00 a.m. to 4:00 p.m. Greenhouse open Tuesday and Thursday from 10:00 a.m. to 3:00 p.m. and Sunday from 11:00 a.m. to 4:00 p.m. Admission free.

For More Information:
Santa Barbara Botanic Garden
1212 Mission Canyon Road
Santa Barbara, CA 93105
(805) 682-4726

Flower Fields

Lompoc

*The flower is the poetry of reproduction. It is
an example of the eternal seductiveness of life.*
— JEAN GIRAUDOUX

 ORE THAN 50 percent of the world's flower seeds
come from the Lompoc Valley, where the cool,
moist summers are ideal for growing flowers. The
fields begin blooming in May, but visit from mid-
June through July to see them at their best.

You'll find fields of pale blue or white alyssum, dahlia,
gazania, lobelia, marigold, verbena, geranium, and delphinium
in shades of blue, pink, rose, and white along Purísima Road
between Rucker Road and Highway 246. Most of the other fields
flank Central Avenue (alyssum, white and purple candytuft,
delphinium, lobelia, marigold, petunia, stock, and sweet pea)
and the railroad tracks between Leege and Floradale avenues
(alyssum, candytuft, delphinium, gazania, deep blue lobelia,
marigold, nasturtium, and pink, purple, and white sweet pea).
Take Ocean Avenue up to the observation point for an excellent
overview of the valley.

Your best bet is to get an up-to-date map from the Lompoc
Valley Chamber of Commerce. (Lompoc Valley is attracting a lot
of businesses and residences; the flower fields are slowly diminishing.) Armed with this
self-guided tour, you
can travel through the
valley at your own pace
and stop to admire the
flowers whenever you
wish. Keep in mind
that this is private
property—don't pick
the flowers (you'll be

Sweet peas.

tempted!), don't walk in the fields, and please keep your vehicle on the paved roads.

Location:
Throughout the Lompoc Valley.

Hours and Admission:
Open to view year round, but best seen from mid-June through July in the cool of early morning when the flowers are at their freshest. Admission free.

For More Information:
Lompoc Valley Chamber of Commerce
111 South "I" Street
Lompoc, CA 93436
(805) 736-4567

La Purísima Mission

Lompoc

*Teach your children
what we have taught our children—
that the earth is our mother.*   — CHIEF SEATTLE

HE GARDENS at La Purísima Mission are not the main attraction, but they're interesting nevertheless. The early natives and padres used all the plants you see for food, medicine, clothing, and tools. Spanish bayonet (*Yucca baccata*) supplied fibers for bowstrings and fishing nets. Crushed toyon berries (*Heteromeles arbutifolia*) went into a cider drink. The peeled bark of the coffeeberry plant (*Rhamnus californica*) provided a laxative. Pomegranates, not only good to eat, made a delicious beverage. Their rinds were used in medicine, and the rinds and flowers together produced a red dye.

A large circular fountain marks the garden area. Pepper and

A circular fountain marks the garden area.

olive trees, the herb garden, and the rest spread out from this point. Look closely at the ground as you walk near the fountain. You may spot a brightly colored red-haired velvet ant (*Dasymutilla coccineohirta*). This pretty little creature may resemble a true ant, but don't pick it up for a closer look—it's actually a form of wasp, with a wasplike sting.

Many butterflies flutter in and around the herb garden, where oregano, dwarf thyme, chives, fern tansy, borage, rue, lemon geranium, and English mint grow. Both the anise swallowtail (*Papilio zelicaon*) and the darker short-tailed black swallowtail (*P. indra*) frequent the wetter areas, sipping nectar from the mint.

Blue butterflies attracted to clover include the little eastern tailed blue (*Everes comyntas*), the larger eastern tailed blue (*E. amyntula*), and the Acmon blue (*Icarica acmon*). Look near the ceanothus plants for the spring azure (*Celastrina ladon*), one of the most common butterflies in the garden area.

The combination of open grassy areas and wooded spots appeals to a wide variety of birds. Expect to see killdeer and red-tailed hawks, roadrunners and western bluebirds, western meadowlarks and scrub jays, rufous hummingbirds and dark-eyed juncos. Visit the mission in winter and spring, and you're likely to see American goldfinches. Also, according to Vernon L. Human's excellent booklet, *Birds of La Purisima Mission*, "a red-shouldered hawk regularly nests in a garden sycamore tree, and a great horned owl annually brings forth its brood from a nest box in a building window." You can purchase this booklet at the mission gift shop.

Overhead, swifts and swallows swoop and dart. Cliff swallows' nests plaster the upper walls of several mission buildings.

Location:
In the Lompoc Valley on Purísima Road.

Hours and Admission:
Open daily from 9:00 a.m. to 5:00 p.m. Admission free.

For More Information:
La Purísima Mission
State Historic Park
2295 Purísima Road
Lompoc, CA 93436
(805) 733-3713

Montaña de Oro
State Park
Los Osos

I will make a palace fit for you and me
Of green days in forests and blue days at sea.
— ROBERT LOUIS STEVENSON

 ROM THE SEA, the profusion of California poppies, tidytips, and California buttercups blooming on the hillsides made it look like a *montaña de oro*—or "mountain of gold." An exciting blend of sea and land, this coastal park mixes wild waves pounding on jagged rocks, smooth flower-filled meadows, and tall rolling hills.

Established as a state park in 1965, the 7,000 acres encompass

Golden flowers dot the ocean bluffs.

Valencia Peak (1,345 feet high), two year-round creeks, and 2.5 miles of rugged California coastline. The animals and plants vary with the terrain. You'll see black oystercatchers at the water's edge and acorn woodpeckers in the higher elevations. California poppies bloom in wide open fields above the ocean while black cottonwoods and California live oaks dot the hillsides. From sea lions at sea level to mountain lions in the hills, the range is great indeed.

Park Highlights

Nature Trails

Trails branching off from the eucalyptus-lined access road take you down to the ocean through meadows of California poppy (*Eschscholzia californica*), mustard, mariposa lily, morning glory, and tidytips. At the shoreline, hottentot fig, yarrow, sand verbena, and sea fig proliferate. Corallina Cove abounds with tidepool life: gooseneck barnacles, anemones, sea stars, sea urchins, and periwinkles.

Nature trails also lead into the hills from the access roads, through wooded valleys and canyons, past streams and a small waterfall along Islay Creek. California live oak, chamise, California sage, monkey-flower, and a stand of Bishop pine (on the slopes south of Coon Creek) grow along the trails. Rare Pecho manzanita highlights the Coon Creek Trail. From October through March, take a look in the eucalyptus trees in the canyons—often the wintering grounds for thousands of monarch butterflies (*Danaus plexippus*).

Birds

Shore birds include cormorants, oystercatchers, willets, and brown pelicans. Head toward the hills to find Allen's, Anna's, and rufous hummingbirds; acorn woodpeckers—which you'll probably hear before you see—shrikes, and common flickers; and screech, barn, and great horned owls. Keen-eyed birders may spot the uncommon rufous-crowned sparrow on south-facing chaparral hillsides.

Mammals

Look just offshore for California and Steller sea lions. Inland you'll see mule deer, black-tailed jackrabbits, coyotes, gray foxes, and perhaps a mountain lion. Blacktail deer browse in the chapparal in the early morning and late afternoon. Grizzly bears once inhabited the region. No more.

Reptiles

Rare two-stripe garter snakes, gopher snakes, California ring-necked snakes, rubber boas, and Pacific rattlesnakes all frequent the park.

Location:
Three miles south of Los Osos on Pecho Road.

Hours and Admission:
Open dawn to dusk. Admission free.

For More Information:
San Luis Obispo Coast Area
Department of Parks and Recreation
20-A Higuera Street
San Luis Obispo, CA 93401
(805) 528-0513

Hearst Castle

San Simeon

The way God would have done it if he had had the money.   — GEORGE BERNARD SHAW

E PREPARED to look up when visiting Hearst San Simeon State Historical Monument. You begin by traveling up a winding oleander-lined road—1,600 feet up to where Hearst Castle crowns a hilltop, above the fog line overlooking the sea. Once you arrive at the mansion, your eyes continue upward to tall Hispano-Mooresque towers. Inside, your eyes again move up to take in the immense tapestries and ornate designs of the ceilings.

Dark green Italian cypresses and tall slender palms also lead your eye skyward, as if competing with the architectural heights. Not to be outdone, groves of towering pines and cedars dot other hillsides rising above you.

The castle stars as the main attraction at La Cuesta Encantada ("The Enchanted Hill"). But plants and gardens do provide a necessary anchor to all this lofty grandeur. Winter-blooming camellias, rhododendrons in the spring, perennials, and year-round annuals spill from planters and line terraces, pools, and pathways. Oleanders, citrus trees, pomegranates, and roses add to the color and fragrance. Native California live oaks, eucalyptus trees, pines, and cedars near the buildings and over the hills help to soften the look of the architecture and provide shade for the exotic animals that run wild.

Wildlife varies from what a ranger refers to as "the great tarantula migration" to huge sambar deer (*Cervus unicolor*) to golden eagles and zebras. Tarantulas don't really migrate; every year in September or October they emerge from underground to mate. If you're lucky (?) you may spot one or two of the large hairy spiders.

William Randolph Hearst kept quite a menagerie of animals at the villa. When ill health forced him to leave, he donated most of them to zoos. A few, however, continued to roam free, and you'll see some of their descendants here and there. Visitors can often spot white fallow deer and Barbary sheep or aoudads (*Ammotragus lervia*). A baby zebra was seen recently. Raccoons, foxes, coyotes, and wild boars live in the area as well.

Hearst Castle offers four different tours. First-timers should definitely take Tour One for a good overview of the buildings and grounds. The true garden lover, however, will also want to take Tour Four. It includes a number of the buildings, but also most of the formal and informal plantings around the villa. When you make reservations, be sure to ask whether Tour Four is available—it's offered only part of the year.

Location:
Off California Highway 1, just east of San Simeon.

Hours and Admission:
Open daily from 8:20 a.m. to 3:20 p.m.; closed Thanksgiving, December 25, and January 1. Admission fee. Call for reservations four weeks in advance: within California, MISTIX (800) 444-7275; outside the state, (619) 425-1950.

For More Information:
Hearst Castle
750 Hearst Castle Road
P.O. Box 8
San Simeon, CA 93452
(805) 927-2020

University of California, Santa Cruz Arboretum

Santa Cruz

There are tides of life as well as tides in the sea.   — EDWIN WAY TEALE

 OME GARDENS are meticulously cared for—everything trimmed, clipped, and kept in its place, never a weed in sight. The UCSC Arboretum is not one of those gardens.

A number of times I followed pathways that just disappeared, leaving me to make my own way. There's a certain exhilaration in the freedom. I could crash through the underbrush without guilt, and the plants living there were free to grow their own way.

The arboretum has one of the finest collections of Australian plants in the world and a superb display of New Zealand and South African plants. The plantings around the parking lot and entrance belie this reputation, however, featuring California plants such as poppy, flannel bush, lupine, and manzanita along with herbs and succulents like *Aloe reitzii*. Visit anytime from March to early April to see the blooming plants at their peak.

Throughout the grounds you'll come upon the silvery, pinkish blue *Acacia baileyana* and bright silver *Leucadendron argenteum*. The banksias and proteas are spectacular, especially the feathery dark purple and light pink *Protea laurifolia* and the furry-edged *P. nerifolia,* Pink Mink.

Because of its proximity to Natural Bridges, a well-known monarch butterfly habitat, lots of the big orange and black creatures flutter through the garden. They join cabbage butterflies (*Papilio rapae*), American painted ladies, red admirals, and northern checkerspots (*Chlosyne palla*). If you're lucky, you may see the lesser unsilvered fritillary (*Speyeria egleis adiaste*), whose population is rapidly diminishing.

Painted Lady.

Hummingbirds love the red and cream flowers of woolly grevillea (*Grevillea lanigera*). And lots of California quail live in the gardens' 150 acres along with brown towhees and flickers.

Location:
On the University of California, Santa Cruz campus via the Empire Grade.

Hours and Admission:
Open daily from 9:00 a.m. to 5:00 p.m. Admission free.

For More Information:
Arboretum Associates
University of California
Santa Cruz, CA 95064
(408) 427-2998

Stewart Orchids
Carpinteria

THIS COMMERCIAL ORCHID NURSERY—which ships flowers world-wide—invites the public to stop by and look around or arrange for group tours in advance. Open weekdays from 8:00 a.m. to 4:00 p.m.; Saturday 10:00 a.m. to 4:00 p.m.; Sunday noon to 4:00 p.m. Admission free. For more information, contact Stewart Orchids, 3376 Foothill Road, Carpinteria, CA 93013. Or call (805) 684-5448.

Santa Barbara Orchid Estate
Santa Barbara

FIVE ACRES of orchids from all over the world include thousands of phalaenopsis plants, cymbidiums, paphiopedilums, and cattleyas. You'll always find something blooming here, no matter what time you visit. Open Monday through Saturday from 8:00 a.m. to 4:30 p.m.; Sunday 10:00 a.m. to 4:00 p.m. Admission free. For more information, contact

Tables loaded with orchids.

Santa Barbara Orchid Estate, 1250 Orchid Drive, Santa Barbara, CA 93111. Or call (805) 967-1284.

Santa Barbara Mission
Santa Barbara

A MORETON BAY fig tree planted in 1890 highlights the mission grounds. Throughout you'll find trumpet vine, cassia, honeysuckle, and lots of bougainvillea. Across the lawn in front of the mission rests the A.C. Postel Memorial Rose Garden, where several beds of labeled roses include the silvery lavender Blue

A.C. Postel Memorial Rose Garden.

Nile and the bright red Show Biz. Acorn woodpeckers dash through the surrounding trees. Open Monday through Saturday and holidays (except Easter, Thanksgiving, and December 25) from 9:00 a.m. to 5:00 p.m.; Sunday 1:00 to 5:00 p.m. Admission fee. For more information, contact Mission Santa Barbara, East Los Olivos and Upper Laguna Streets, Santa Barbara, CA 93101. Or call (805) 682-4713.

Alice Keck Park
Memorial Garden

Santa Barbara

THIS 4.5-ACRE GARDEN brims with native trees, plants, and ground covers. Flower beds emphasize certain colors, such as pink in one section, blue in another. Hundreds of koi swim about in a large pond, surrounded by expanses of lawn and over 100 flowering trees and palms. Open daily from dawn to dusk. Admission free. For more information, contact the City of Santa Barbara Parks Department, 402 E. Ortega Street, Santa Barbara, CA 93102. Or call (805) 564-5433.

Lotusland

Santa Barbara

THE 37-ACRE ESTATE of the late Ganna Walska holds a fantastic collection of euphorbias, cacti, dragon trees (*Dracena draco*), queen palms, Chilean wine palms, and cycads. A large commercial nursery in the 1800s, the gardens were haphazardly laid out and delightfully planted. Blue-green slag glass from Coca-Cola bottles lines garden beds and pathways, an enormous cymbidium orchid grows in an old whaling pot, and water bubbles from a fountain made of giant clamshells.

Paths take you past a striking bunya-bunya tree (*Araucaria bidwellii*), orchards, and a pond that attracts great blue and green herons, great egrets, and kingfishers. Red-shouldered hawks, great horned owls, robins, acorn woodpeckers, and hummingbirds swoop and dart. The estate's signature lotus plants bloom in July and August.

Lotusland welcomes only approved groups with horticultural or botanical affiliations and advance reservations, but regular hours and fees for public tours are being planned. For more information, contact Lotusland, 695 Ashley Road, Santa Barbara, CA 93108. Or call (805) 969-3767.

A stone lantern sits next to a lily pond.

Shin-Zen "Friendship" Garden
Fresno

THIS THREE-ACRE GARDEN celebrates the four seasons with cherry trees and bulbs blooming in the spring; shady trees breaking the heat of the summer sun; Japanese maples and liquidamber turning copper, red, and gold in fall; and a stand of pines representing winter.

Small streams lined with white alders, tulip trees, and coast redwoods run through the garden. Weeping willows grace the water's edge. Located in Woodward Park, the grounds also feature a koi pond, stone lanterns, and little bridges. Open weekends from 10:00 a.m. to dusk. For more information, contact Shin-Zen "Friendship" Garden, Highway 41 and Friant Road, Fresno, CA 93636. Or call (209) 488-1551.

Duncan Water Gardens
Fresno

KOI PONDS, waterfalls, and objects of art by local artists fill this 3.5-acre private garden. Black swans swim on a pond bordered by Japanese maples, camellias, azaleas, and magnolias. Open Tuesday through Saturday from 9:00 a.m. to 5:00 p.m; Sunday 10:00 a.m. to 4:00 p.m (except holidays). Admission free. For more information, contact Duncan Water Gardens, 691 Temperance Avenue, Fresno, CA 93727. Or call (209) 255-7233.

Goldsmith Seeds, Inc.
Gilroy

ROWS AND SQUARES of various flowers in different colors block out the extensive lawn area fronting Goldsmith Seeds, a wholesale seed company. Plan to see the stunning rainbow effect at its height from June through September. Pansies bloom in winter and reach their peak in March and April. Open daily from dawn to dusk. Admission free. For more information, contact Gold-smith Seeds, Inc., 2280 Hecker Pass Highway, P.O. Box 1349, Gilroy, CA 95021. Or call (408) 847-7333.

Mission San Carlos Borromeo del Río Carmelo

Carmel

FLOWERS BLOOM even in the middle of January at this beautiful mission, but in late March or early April the grounds practically vibrate with color. Crimson bougainvillea predominates, accentuated nicely with pale purple wisteria, the yellow flowers of cassia, and the big floppy-petaled blossoms of matilija poppy. Open Monday through Saturday from 9:30 a.m. to 4:30 p.m.; Sunday and holidays 10:30 a.m. to 4:30 p.m. For more information, contact

Carmel Mission.

Mission San Carlos Borromeo del Río Carmelo, 3080 Rio Road, Carmel, CA 93921. Or call (408) 624-3600.

Casa Amesti

Monterey

A PRIVATE men's club leases Casa Amesti from its owner, the National Trust for Historic Preservation. Gardens around the restored 1834 adobe concentrate on formality, symmetry, and subdued color provided by succulents, ivies, ferns, and wisteria. Open weekends from 2:00 to 4:00 p.m. (except July). Admission fee. For more information, contact Casa Amesti, 516 Polk Street, Monterey, CA 93940. Or call (408) 372-2608.

Henry W. Coe State Park
Morgan Hill

COVERING more than 32,000 acres, Henry W. Coe State Park makes a wonderful place to visit in spring when entire meadows bloom with wild flowers. You'll see golden orange California poppies, shooting stars, purplish blue lupine, mariposa lilies, and owl's clover. Red-tailed hawks and turkey vultures soar overhead. With luck you may even spot a golden eagle. California quail, acorn woodpeckers, and western bluebirds live closer to the ground.

The park lies 14 miles east of Morgan Hill on East Dunne Avenue. Get there early—the parking lot fills quickly. Open year round. Admission fee. For more information, contact Henry W. Coe State Park, P.O. Box 846, Morgan Hill, CA 95038. Or call (408) 779-2728.

Antonelli Begonia Gardens
Santa Cruz

THIS POPULAR nursery offers tours from June through September, but try to time your visit between August and September when the tuberous begonias reach their peak. Blooms cascading from baskets range from deep red and orange to yellow, pink, and creamy white. Of special note: the big roselike blossoms of the aptly named Begonia of Distinction. Open daily from 9:00 a.m. to 5:00 p.m. Admission free. For more information, contact Antonelli Begonia Gardens, 2545 Capitola Road, Santa Cruz, CA 95010. Or call (408) 475-5222.

Red-tailed hawk.

Arboretum of the University of California, Davis, *Davis*

Azalea State Reserve, *Arcata*

Berkeley Municipal Rose Garden, *Berkeley*

Blake Garden, *Kensington*

Capitol Park, *Sacramento*

Conservatory of Flowers, *San Francisco*

Dunsmuir House and Garden, *Oakland*

Filoli, *Woodside*

Hakone Japanese Garden, *Saratoga*

Japanese Friendship Garden and Teahouse, *San Jose*

Japanese Tea Garden & Tea House, *San Francisco*

John McLaren Memorial Rhododendron Dell, *San Francisco*

Kruse Rhododendron State Reserve Plantation, *Jenner*

Lakeside Park Garden, *Oakland*

Luther Burbank Home and Memorial Gardens, *Santa Rosa*

Mendocino Coast Botanical Gardens, *Fort Bragg*

Micke Grove Park Japanese Garden, *Lodi*

Overfelt Botanical Gardens, *San Jose*

Regional Parks Botanic Garden, *Oakland*

San Mateo Japanese Garden, *San Mateo*

Strybing Arboretum and Botanical Gardens, *San Francisco*

University of California, Berkeley Botanical Garden, *Berkeley*

Villa Montalvo Arboretum, *Saratoga*

Villa Montalvo Arboretum

Saratoga

The first purple wisteria
I recall from boyhood hung
on a wire outside the windows
of the breakfast room next door....

— *PHILIP LEVINE*

 NCE THE SUMMER home of San Francisco mayor and U.S. Senator James D. Phelan, Villa Montalvo now serves as a center for fine arts. The Mediterranean-style villa took shape in 1912. It commands the top of a knoll overlooking lawns, hedges, trees, and the surrounding foothills of the Santa Cruz Mountains. John McLaren, who helped design Golden Gate Park, designed these formal gardens.

Wisteria headlines the show in April. It drapes sensuously across the terraces of the Front Veranda, Oval Garden, and Pavilion with flowers in shades of white, lavender, and purple. Big full hydrangea bushes decorate the Oval Garden with white, pink, and lavender blooms from May through July.

Phelan imported trees and plants from around the world to beautify his estate. Yellow-flowering black, star, and Bailey acacias bloom in January along the drive leading to the front lawn. Red horsechestnuts (*Aesculus carnea* Briotii) bloom with pink flowers in spring along with the waxy white flowers of *Magnolia grandiflora* and *M. soulangiana* (March). Cypresses, birches, valley oaks, and bunya-bunya trees appear throughout.

Bright patches of color erupt from January through April thanks to plum trees, camellias, azaleas, rhododendrons, and several varieties of daffodils. In June, look for the orange blossoms of the cape honeysuckle vine near the villa kitchen.

Designated an Audubon Society bird sanctuary, the estate has a number of trails leading into the chaparral and up to a number of viewpoints. Watch for California quail, Steller jays, and woodpeckers, deer, squirrels, lizards, and opossums.

Location:
On Montalvo Road in Saratoga.

Hours and Admission:
Open weekdays from 8:00 a.m. to 5:00 p.m.; weekends and holidays 9:00 a.m. to 5:00 p.m. Admission free.

For More Information:
Villa Montalvo Center for the Arts and Arboretum
15400 Montalvo Road
P.O. Box 158
Saratoga, CA 95071
(408) 741-3421
Arboretum Ranger Station:
(408) 867-0190

Hakone
Japanese Garden
Saratoga

Blossom by blossom the spring begins.
— ALGERNON CHARLES SWINBURNE

N 1918, after visiting gardens in Japan, Isabel Stine employed an Imperial gardener and a Japanese architect to design her garden and residence in the hills above Saratoga. The city's purchase of the estate in 1966 resulted in this lovely and tranquil 15-acre park.

As one of the most authentic Japanese gardens in the state, it

Water lily.

consists of four primary sections. The whole nestles against a steep hillside that creates ever-changing views and perspectives.

The Hill and Pond Garden overlooks a pavilion, waterfall, ponds, and bridge. Japanese red pine and Hinoki cypress complement a dwarf Japanese black pine that grows next to a Momoyama stone lantern on an island in the small pond. Flowering cherry trees create soft pink puffs of color above the waterfall in March and April; red, pink, and white camellias bloom in winter. Large koi in shades of orange, silver, red, and black swim languidly beneath the water's surface. Water lilies bloom from May to October. In April, enjoy an especially pretty view of the pond from the Wisteria Pavilion, a building draped in pale lavender flowers.

The Tea Garden instills a feeling of serenity with its moss garden, water basin, and stepping-stones. Japanese maples, turning a golden rusty red in fall, separate the Tea Garden from the Zen Garden, where azaleas add a touch of color to an otherwise monochromatic landscape of raked gravel, deliberately placed rocks, and stone lanterns.

Kizuna-En (the Bamboo Garden) features many fine examples of the fast-growing grass. The Japan Bamboo Society of

Saratoga maintains the plants and looks forward to a Bamboo Research Center in the future.

Write to the City of Saratoga to arrange for a group tour.

Location:
On Big Basin Way, off Highway 9 in Saratoga.

Hours and Admission:
Open weekdays from 10:00 a.m. to 5:00 p.m.; weekends from 11:00 a.m. to 5:00 p.m.; closed holidays. Admission free; donation suggested.

For More Information:
City of Saratoga
13777 Fruitvale Avenue
Saratoga, CA 95070
or
Hakone Japanese Gardens
21000 Big Basin Way
Saratoga, CA 95070
(408) ~~867-3438~~ (408) 741-4994

Japanese Friendship Garden and Teahouse

San Jose

All are nothing but flowers
In a flowering universe. — NAKAGAWA SOEN-ROSHI

 TRADITIONAL Japanese garden encourages you to slow down, look around, and quietly appreciate the symbolism in the smallest things. Take this garden, for example, where irises next to the entrance symbolize purity, innocence, and chastity. The five tiers of a pagoda

Daisies.

represent the five elements: earth, wind, fire, water, and metal. And the waterfall represents a wise deity who reveals his wisdom if you listen closely to the rushing water.

The pine trees—usually bearing two needles per bract—suggest conjugal love. A large rock placed next to a small one represents a father teaching or talking to his son. Leave your worries behind on the zigzag bridge—bad spirits cannot zig and zag; they travel only in straight lines.

The garden provides a pocket of serenity within rambunctious Kelley Park. Paths urge you gently along past a series of ponds with water lilies, irises growing in tubs here and there, stone lanterns, cedars and redwoods, beeches and birches, rhododendrons and azaleas. Koi—representing long life—greet you enthusiastically when you offer the food available for purchase. The garden brought in more than 3,000 koi from Japan in 1966. Because koi live for 35 or 40 years, some of the fish you see may be part of this original, well-traveled group.

A cherry orchard blooms with delicate pink and white flowers in the spring. According to the garden brochure, the flowers symbolize loyalty to country, family, and friends: "It is said that an individual blossom is insignificant but the entire tree is complete and beautiful." Plantings of daisies, sago palms, lacy-leaved Japanese maples, and crape myrtle add a variety of colors, textures, and shapes to the gardens.

Location:
Off Highway 101 in San Jose.

Hours and Admission:
Open daily from 10:00 a.m. to dusk. Admission free.

For More Information:
Japanese Friendship Garden and Teahouse
1390 Senter Road
San Jose, CA 95100
(408) 292-8188

Overfelt Botanical Gardens

San Jose

It will be a place of beauty with trees, lawns, shrubbery and other facilities and improvements designed or planned to provide a place of rest, relaxation, aesthetic and other enjoyment for the people of San Jose.

— MILDRED OVERFELT

ITH THESE WORDS, Mildred Overfelt deeded 33 acres of land to the City of San Jose, hoping that good would come of it. Good *has* come of it. As you enter the gardens, you're immediately surrounded by rolling lawns, well-kept flower gardens, and leafy green trees. Ducks (mostly mallards) swim about in three ponds; hummingbirds (Anna's) zip from flower to flower; and redwinged blackbirds cling to swaying reeds. Overfelt's desire for a place of rest, relaxation, and enjoyment has been fulfilled.

Wild flowers along the shores of the ponds include the red, poppylike clarkia (*Clarkia concinna*), flax (*Linum usitatissimum*), California poppy (*Eschscholzia californica*), sweet alyssum (*Lobularia maritima*), and baby blue-eyes (*Nemophila menziesii*).

Pathways lead through an arbor featuring box elder (*Acer negundo*), coast live oak (*Quercus agrifolia*), flowering plum (*Prunus atropurpurea*), and California buckeye (*Aesculus californica*). In other parts of the gardens you'll find a Chinese scholar tree (*Sophora japonica*) and a plane tree (*Platanus orientalis*). A gift from the people of Greece, this plane tree descends from the one under which Hippocrates taught medicine on the island of Kos in the fifth century B.C.

A large part of the garden celebrates Chinese culture. You enter the Chinese section through a beautiful Friendship Gate

Bronze statue of Confucius.

and walk along pathways past a 15-foot marble and bronze statue of Confucius, the orange-roofed Chiang Kai-Shek Pavilion, and the elaborately carved dragons, fairies, and lions of Sun Yat-Sen Memorial Hall.

The gardens serve as a sanctuary for wildlife; so in addition to various birds, you may spot jackrabbits, ground squirrels, and toads, bullfrogs, and crayfish in or near the water. The ponds are particularly good for birders in winter, when migratory birds stop off to rest along their journey.

Butterflies too love all this water combined with grass, trees, plants, and flowers. You may see lots of large, handsomely colored swallowtails, especially near the lakes. Examples include the pipevine (*Battus philenor*), anise (*Papilio zelicaon*), western (*Pterourus rutulus*), two-tailed (*P. multicaudatus*), and pale tiger (*P. eurymedon*) varieties. The moister areas attract coppers as well: the tailed copper (*Tharsalea arota*), great gray copper (*Gaeides xanthoides*), gorgon copper (*G. gorgon*), and purplish copper (*Epidemia helloides*).

If you see a flash of blue, it may be the echo blue butterfly (*Celastrina ladon echo*). Look for it near the oaks and California buckeye trees. The familiar painted lady (*Vanessa cardui*), American painted lady (*V. virginiensis*), west coast lady (*V. annabella*), red admiral (*V. atalanta rubria*), and buckeye (*Junonia coenia*) abound. And, of course, the regal monarch (*Danaus plexippus*) also swoops through the garden.

San Jose's Department of Parks and Recreation offers guided group tours by prearrangement.

Location:
At Park Drive and McKee Road, adjacent to the San Jose Public Library.

Hours and Admission:
Open daily from 10:00 a.m. to sunset; closed January 1 and December 25. Admission free.

For More Information:
Overfelt Botanical Gardens
City of San Jose
Department of Parks and Recreation
151 W. Mission Street
San Jose, CA 95110
(408) 251-3323

San Mateo Japanese Garden
San Mateo

Adopt the pace of nature: her secret is patience.
— RALPH WALDO EMERSON

 ATURE LIVE OAKS and cork oaks lining the pathway to the entrance create a sense of anticipation for what lies behind the wooden walls. Inside, you're immediately greeted with a large pond, fountain, waterfall, and meticulously clipped and trimmed trees at water's edge. Visit in spring and fall to do the garden justice; any other time merely whets your appetite.

In springtime, purple and white irises, pink and red azaleas and rhododendrons, flowering cherries, and plums add pizzazz

A rock-lined path leads to the teahouse.

to this little garden. In autumn, the fiery gold, yellow, and crimson leaves of liquidamber, Japanese maple, and red Japanese maple reflect brilliantly in the water. Large koi add another touch of color as they swarm around the pond's surface every day at mealtime, 11:00 a.m. and 3:00 p.m.

A path around the water's perimeter takes you over small bridges past a variety of stone lanterns. An offshore island features Japanese red pine and a weeping Japanese apricot.

Location:
In Central Park at the corner of Laurel and Fifth avenues in downtown San Mateo.

Hours and Admission:
Open weekdays from 9:00 a.m. to 4:00 p.m., weekends and holidays from 11:00 a.m. to 5:00 p.m. Admission free.

For More Information:
City of San Mateo
330 W. 20th Ave.
San Mateo, CA 94403-1388
(415) 377-4700

Filoli

Woodside

Time Began in a Garden — SUNDIAL AT FILOLI

 F YOU COULD SEE the gardens of Filoli from the air, you might think of a stained-glass window. Indeed, you may have seen them—the mansion and its grounds starred in the opening helicopter shot of the television series "Dynasty."

Trim, geometrically shaped, clearly delineated gardens cover 16 acres of land around a handsome brick mansion. Built between 1916 and 1919 for William Bourn, a utility magnate and heir to a gold rush fortune, the acronymic name comes from Bourn's credo: To Fight, to Love, to Live. Filoli now belongs to the National Trust for Historic Preservation. The gardens reach their peak in April and May but, because of devoted and constant care, are delightful to visit *any* time of year.

Garden Highlights

Entry Courtyard

Magnolia trees and Japanese maples line the driveway and front courtyard, backed by coast live oaks and atlas cedars (*Cedrus atlantica*).

Sunken Garden

Brick steps descend to a rectangular pool in the Sunken Garden, where water lilies bloom. Look for the white cat who sometimes sits poolside. Delicately trimmed gray-green olive trees, magnolias, and yews provide contrasting color and form.

Walled Garden

The Chartres Cathedral Garden replicates a stained-glass window with colorful flower beds (the stained glass) lined with boxwood borders (the lead outlines). A lush *Ginkgo biloba* grows here along with New Zealand beech trees (*Nothofagus solandri*) and *Pittosporum tenuifolium*.

Irises and wolly lamb's ears line a garden walkway.

Woodland Garden

Rhododendrons, azaleas, and camellias as big as trees (*Camellia japonica*) enjoy the filtered sunlight below tall oaks and Japanese maples. Shade-loving redwood sorrel (*Oxalis oregana*) and bridal wreath (*Francoa ramosa*) also thrive.

Rose Garden

Notice the silvery pink flowers of Silver Spoon, the climbing rose Kathleen with its pinkish white petals and yellow interiors, and Double Delight with its dark pink petal tips accenting the lighter pink flower.

Knot Garden

Long narrow plantings of crimson barberry, lavender, gray santolina, and horehound crisscross one another to give the impression of thick ropes wound over and under in a series of knots.

Tours

The public (except children under 12) may visit any Friday and the first Saturday and second Sunday of every month without prior arrangements. Otherwise, with a reservation, you can join a guided three-mile nature hike of the grounds or a two-hour tour of the first floor of the 43-room modified Georgian-style mansion and 16 acres of formal gardens. Mansion and garden tours begin Tuesday through Saturday at 10:00 a.m. and 1:00 p.m.

Location:
Off Highway 280 to Edgewood Road, then west on Cañada Road.

Hours and Admission:
Open designated days from 10:00 a.m. to 2:00 p.m. Admission fee.

For More Information:
Filoli
Cañada Road
Woodside, CA 94062
(415) 366-4640
Reservations: (415) 364-2880

Conservatory of Flowers
San Francisco

The coldest winter I ever spent was a summer in San Francisco. — MARK TWAIN

 O MATTER how cold San Francisco's summers get, it's always warm inside the Conservatory of Flowers, where whitewashed glass panes keep in the sun's warmth. A misting system, designed to provide a rain-forest environment, keeps the humidity up. Exotic calathea, epiphyllum, cyclamen, palm, and papyrus delight in the warm and humid atmosphere.

The conservatory presents roughly three sections. Philoden-drons, palms, and vines lead your eye skyward in the tall, domed central area. To your left, the west wing displays ever-changing

Exotic plants thrive in the east wing.

exhibits of seasonal flowers. Lilies bloom at Easter, poinsettias during the Christmas season. To your right, in the east wing's steamier, mistier, more exotic section, water lilies, ferns, and bromeliads soak up the heat and moisture.

Location:
Opposite the John McLaren Memorial Rhododendron Dell on Kennedy Drive in the northeast section of Golden Gate Park.

Hours and Admission:
Open daily from 9:00 a.m. to 5:00 p.m. Admission fee.

For More Information:
San Francisco Recreation and Parks
McLaren Lodge
Golden Gate Park
Fell and Stanyan Streets
San Francisco, CA 94117
(415) 666-7017

Japanese Tea Garden & Tea House

San Francisco

Loveliest of trees, the cherry now
Is hung with bloom along the bough.
— A. E. HOUSEMAN

 RIGINALLY designed as a Japanese village for the 1894 Mid-Winter Exposition, the garden has been enlarged and redesigned. It continues as one of the most popular spots in Golden Gate Park.

From the carved Hinoki cypress gate at the entrance, pathways take you up a gradual incline where a bright red-orange pagoda, torii, and temple gate dominate the upper slopes. Below lie a beautifully kept dwarf conifer collection, carved stone lanterns, a series of ponds, small waterfalls, and an arched bridge. Flowering cherry trees, azaleas, and rhododendrons celebrate spring; crimson, copper, and gold leaves of Japanese maples brighten autumn; and camellias and flowering magnolia trees add delicate touches of pink, red, and white in winter.

Japenese Tea Garden Pagoda.

Location:
On Hagiwara Tea Garden Drive at Martin Luther King Drive in Golden Gate Park.

Hours and Admission:
Open daily from 9:00 a.m. to 5:00 p.m. Teahouse service from 10:30 a.m. to 4:30 p.m. Admission fee waived the first Wednesday of each month.

For More Information:
San Francisco Recreation and Parks
McLaren Lodge
Golden Gate Park
Fell and Stanyan Streets
San Francisco, CA 94117
(415) 752-1171

John McLaren Memorial Rhododendron Dell

San Francisco

Look, in short, at practically anything—the coot's foot, the mantis's face, a banana, the human ear—and see that not only did the creator create everything, but that he is apt to create anything. He'll stop at nothing.

—ANNIE DILLARD

 OHN MCLAREN, the first superintendent and architect of Golden Gate Park, particularly loved rhododendrons. Knowing these moisture- and mist-loving plants would do especially well in the park, he set about upping the count from 7 kinds of rhododendrons in 1887 to the current number of 500 types today.

The rhododendrons peak from late March through May.

The delightfully undisciplined garden sprawls over 18 acres. None of the 3,500 rhododendron plants bear labels, nor do the pathways that run hither and thither through the dell. Expect a visual and emotional experience rather than a methodical scientific outing. In late March through early May, the colors, scents, cool mists, and sensuality of the dell can overwhelm you. Pink Pearl rhododendrons surround a statue of John McLaren at the entrance to the gardens.

Location:
Opposite the Conservatory of Flowers on Kennedy Drive in the northeast section of Golden Gate Park.

Hours and Admission:
Open from dawn to dusk. Admission fee.

For More Information:
San Francisco Recreation and Parks
McLaren Lodge
Golden Gate Park
Fell and Stanyan Streets
San Francisco, CA 94117
(415) 666-7200

Strybing Arboretum and Botanical Gardens

San Francisco

The butterfly counts not months but moments,
and has time enough. — RABIN-DRANATH TAGORE

 EVENTY acres of lawns, ponds, enormous trees, stands of rhododendrons, and pockets of specialty gardens welcome you at Strybing Arboretum and Botanical Gardens in Golden Gate Park. Even with a map the gardens can be confusing, so be sure to pick up a brochure at the entrance. You'll find this seasonal publication specifically oriented toward what's in bloom and spectacular at the time. It's invaluable for seeing the best the arboretum has to offer—which is considerable!

The main entry greets you in spring with the pink flowers of New Zealand tea tree (*Leptospermum scoparium* Helene Strybing). From the entrance you see enormous trees and a broad expanse of lawn. Tasmanian gum (*Eucalyptus globulus*) grows across from a large Monterey pine (*Pinus radiata*), while a tall Monterey cypress (*Cupressus macrocarpa*) reigns supreme in the center of the lawn.

Garden Highlights

Mediterranean Collections

A variety of tough, leathery manzanitas (Spanish for "little apples"), wild irises, and ceanothus plants grow in the Arthur Menzies Garden of California Native Plants—especially pretty in spring when baby blue-eyes (*Nemophila maculata*) and goldfields (*Lasthenia chrysostoma*) bloom. In fall, a grove of aspen trees (*Populus tremuloides*) turns from cool green to orangish yellow. Look on the California buckeye tree (*Aesculus californica*) for the large seeds—easy to spot once the leaves start to shed in late August.

In the Cape Province Garden you'll find one of the garden's more spectacular plant groups, the *Proteaceae,* including *P. eximia* and the paler pink *P. obtusifolia*. Note the soft, gleaming leaves of the silver trees (*Leucadendron argenteum*). Lots of daisies burst into flower along with aloe, kniphofia, and ice plant in spring.

Protea eximia.

New World Cloud Forest

This garden offers an eerie place to visit on a cool gray morning. A misting system keeps the plants happy while adding to the brooding, primeval atmosphere. Ferns, begonias, bromeliads, epiphytes, and fuchsias reach their peak on the small hillside from late summer through Christmas.

Magnolias

The garden takes justifiable pride in its extensive magnolia collection. It began in 1924 with one tree, a *Magnolia campbellii*. In 1940 this became the first of its type to bloom in the United States, and the flower has since become the arboretum's logo. Twenty of these beauties grow in the arboretum. They stretch 70 feet high and bear flowers as big as dinner plates. Late winter is the best time to see them in full flower, the trunks skirted with pink and white petals that have dropped in profusion to the ground.

Takamine Garden

Japanese flowering cherry (*Prunus serrulata*) and weeping cherry (*P. subhirtilla pendula*) surround a placid little pond. Plants such as *Nuphar polysepalum* from western North America and *Menyanthes trifoliata* bloom in the water. Irises bloom at water's edge. Conifers line the banks. Subtle complementary colors

Main entrance, Strybing Arboretum.

range from the blue-gray needles of *Picea pungens* to the yellow-ish green needles of *Chamaecyparis obtusa*.

Rhododendrons and Camellias

The garden's 900 species of rhododendron and 50 cultivars of camellia present their patches of color from late winter through spring. Tree-sized *Rhododendron arboreum* blooms in January and February with big red flowers. California rosebay (*R. macrophyllum*) and fragrant western azalea (*R. occidentale*) add to the bursts of color. Most of the rhododendrons grow near the north entrance, where you'll also find the unusual yellow and orange flowers of Exbury azaleas.

Birds

American wigeons and coots join the lake's year-round mallard population in fall, winter, and spring. Mew gulls accompany resident Western gulls in winter. Killdeer nest nearby.

American kestrels and red-shouldered hawks fly through all year; they, too, nest in the garden. Allen's hummingbirds flit all over the place in spring and summer, joining permanent Anna's residents. Downy woodpeckers and northern flickers make the garden their year-round home, along with scrub jays, bushtits, and pigmy nuthatches. If you arrive just as the garden opens and head off to the more remote sections, you may catch a covey of California quail scurry-ing through the under-brush.

Butterflies

Big yellow and black western swallowtails sometimes frequent the garden lake and pond areas of the Takamine Garden. Painted ladies

Proteas are clearly labeled.

(*Vanessa cardui*) practically swarm through the grounds in early spring; look in the sunny flower beds at the main entrance. The relatively fearless red admiral (*V. atalanta rubria*) may even land on your shirt, while a large monarch (*Danaus plexippus*) flutters lazily nearby.

Tours and Resources

The arboretum offers guided tours daily at 1:30 p.m. On week-ends, a morning tour begins at 10:30 a.m. You can visit the Horticultural Library weekdays from 8:00 a.m. to 4:30 p.m. and weekends from 10:00 a.m. to 5:00 p.m.

Location:
At 9th Avenue and Lincoln Way in Golden Gate Park.

Hours and Admission:
Open weekdays from 8:00 a.m. to 4:30 p.m.; weekends and holidays 10:00 a.m. to 5:00 p.m. Admission free.

For More Information:
Strybing Arboretum Society
9th Avenue at Lincoln Way
San Francisco, CA 94122
(415) 661-1316

Dunsmuir House and Garden

Oakland

Watching gardeners label their plants
I vow with all beings
to practice the old horticulture
and let the plants identify me. — ROBERT AITKEN

 UNSMUIR HOUSE, built in 1899, nestles among cedars, Monterey pines, black locust trees, and Japanese yews. Designed in part by John McLaren, who also designed Golden Gate Park, the 48 acres of gardens surrounding the mansion continue the opulent look. A delicate white gazebo sits at the edge of a pond where papyrus, rushes, woodwardia ferns, and bamboo grow. Wisteria and cape honeysuckle drape an arbor area.

Visit the cactus and succulent garden in spring, when the large opuntia, or beavertail cactus, blooms with big red, orange, and pink blossoms. Agave, aloe, echeveria, sedum, and yucca thrive as well. Red-tailed hawks and turkey vultures soar overhead. Quail scrabble about under the bushes.

Location:
On Peralta Oaks Court in Oakland.

Hours and Admission:
Open Sundays only from Easter through mid-September, from noon to 4:00 p.m. Admission free.

For More Information:
Dunsmuir House and Garden
2960 Peralta Oaks Court
Oakland, CA 94605
(510) 562-7588

Lakeside Park Garden
Oakland

Those who wish to pet and baby wild animals "love" them. But those who respect their natures and wish to let them live normal lives, love them more. — EDWIN WAY TEALE

Y THE TIME I reached the garden entrance I had already seen a pair of Canada geese with their chicks, a number of black-crowned night herons, and a great egret. To garden lovers interested in birds, and bird lovers interested in gardens—this is the place for you!

You'll find a little bit of everything: a Japanese garden, desert plants, rhododendrons. There's even a palmetum, maintained by the International Palm Society and considered the most complete collection in Northern California. Examples range from the cool gray Mexican blue palm (*Brahea armata*) to *Trachycarpus wagneranus*, a short fan palm from the Himalayas.

A collection of fuchsias—including Jingle Bells, the deep purple and red Martin's Midnight, and the light purple and pink Randy—delights your eye *and* the eye of an occasional hummingbird. In a planting of irises, the light peach-colored Tahiti Sunrise and the purple and white Circus Stripes compete for attention.

Built in 1870, Lake Merritt across the street is the oldest man-made wildlife refuge in the United States. Birds include Canada geese, great and snowy egrets, canvasbacks, Forster's terns, pintails, lesser scaups, ruddy ducks, and common goldeneyes. You may see white pelicans; and you're almost sure to see

Great egret.

black-crowned night herons, both adults and juveniles, perched in the branches of the sycamore trees.

Location:
Opposite Lake Merritt at Bellevue and Grand avenues.

Hours and Admission:
Open weekdays from 10:00 a.m. to 3:00 p.m. Open weekends and holidays, May through November, from 10:00 a.m. to 5:00 p.m.; closing at 4:00 p.m. the rest of year. Closed January 1, Thanksgiving, and December 25. Admission free, but expect a parking fee on weekends and holidays.

For More Information:
Lakeside Park Garden
666 Bellevue Avenue
Oakland, CA 94612
(510) 273-2197

Regional Parks Botanic Garden
Oakland

Imagine 160,000 square miles of California set in a ten-acre garden that can be walked in a day. — GARDEN BROCHURE

 HIS GARDEN looks small but walks big. Pathways wind and curve and double back on themselves, wander up hillsides, down by little streams, and across bridges. Plantings represent the various regions of California, from seacoast bluffs to arid foothills to coastal mountains and two types of deserts. Walking along the zigzag paths, you find yourself admiring western buttercups in the Shasta Cascade Section at one turn and grizzly bear cactus in the

Southern California Section at another. The collection includes a specimen of every conifer found in the state and almost every oak.

Situated in Wildcat Canyon, a part of Tilden Regional Park in the hills above Oakland and Berkeley, the garden concentrates on collecting and cultivating native California plants. Each of the ten sections showcases the terrain, plants, trees, and flowers of a particular geographical area. Wildcat Creek runs through the center of the gardens.

Autumn leaves cover a garden path.

Valley, Santa Lucia, Franciscan, Channel Islands, Southern California, and Shasta Cascade sections lie on the east side of the creek. Sierran, Redwood, Pacific Rain Forest, and Sea Bluff sections flank the west.

Visit in springtime, when rhododendron, ceanothus, iris, mariposa-tulip, cactus, clarkia, and bush poppy bloom. Or time your visit for fall, when the leaves of cottonwoods, deciduous oaks, dogwoods, willows, and vine maples turn color.

Garden Highlights

Shasta Cascade Section

Near the Visitor Center grow pretty little western buttercups (*Ranunculus occidentalis*), Del Norte manzanitas (*Arctostaphylos columbiana*), and the purple and gold varieties of Del Norte iris (*Iris innominata*). Trees include weeping spruce (*Picea brewerana*), California bay (*Umbellularia californica*), and blackfruit dogwood (*Cornus sessilis*).

Sierran Section

Wild flowers bloom profusely in spring. Varieties include pretty face (*Tritelia ixioides*), purple fairy lantern (*Calochortus amoenus*) from Tulare County, and woolly monkey-flower (*Diplacus calycinus*) from Fresno County.

Pacific Rain Forest Section

Rhododendrons and azaleas flower in the shade of coast wax-myrtle (*Myrica californica*) from Mendocino County, Oregon crab apple (*Malus fusca*) from Humboldt County, and Port Orford cedar (*Chamaecyparis lawsoniana*).

Grizzly bear cactus.

Southern California Section

The rare and endangered San Diego ceanothus (*C. cyaneus*) from Lakeside joins grizzly bear cactus (*Opuntia erinacea*) from the western Mojave Desert and the endangered San Diego grindelia (*G. hallii*) from Julian.

Sea Bluff Section

Rare in California, black crowberry (*Empetrum hermaphroditum*) grows with dwarf juniper (*Juniperus communis*) from Del Norte County and the seldom-seen coast lily (*Lilium maritimum*) from Sonoma County.

Channel Islands Section

Catalina and Santa Cruz ironwood and giant yellow coreopsis (*Coreopsis gigantea*) highlight this section.

Santa Lucia Section

White- and pink-flowering red-skinned onion (*Allium haematochiton*) from San Luis Obispo County, tansy phacelia (*Phacelia tanacetifolia*), and bristlecone fir (*Abies bracteata pinaceae*) line the pathways.

Overview of Regional Parks Botanic Garden.

Birds

Unusual birds spotted in the gardens include the calliope hummingbird (*Stellula calliope*)—the smallest hummer in the United States—and the indigo bunting (*Passerina cyanea*)—extremely rare for this area. The more common birds include rufous-sided towhees (often seen eating the reddish orange berries of the madrone tree), Steller jays, robins, hermit warblers, American dippers, a variety of woodpeckers, and chestnut-sided warblers.

Butterflies

With such a variety of plant life and regional diversity, you can expect numerous types of butterflies. The showiest and most obvious are the monarch (*Danaus plexippus*), the anise swallowtail (*Papilio zelicaon*), and the western tiger swallowtail (*P. rutulus*). Look in the higher elevations for the anise swallowtail, and check the thistle plants in Bed 121 of the Valley Section and milkweed plants in Bed 635 of the Sierra Section for the western tiger swallowtail. The milkweed also attracts mourning cloaks (*Nymphalis antiopa*).

Sara orange-tips (*Anthocharis sara*) are easy to spot if their wings are wide open—they're white with bright reddish orange tips. Wild flowers in early spring attract the painted lady (*Vanessa cardui*), the smaller Acmon blue (*Icarica acmon*), and the boldly colored red admiral (*Vanessa atalanta*).

From April to September you may see the Lorquin's admiral (*Basilarchia lorquini*), a tough little critter known for protecting its territory. It will even drive off birds who dare to invade its space.

Tours and Activities

Regular garden tours begin at 1:30 p.m. at the Visitor Center from June through August. Group tours are available by appointment. At 10:30 a.m. on Saturdays, the garden offers slide shows and lectures on various topics. Sample programs include "How to Build Naturalistic Rock Outcrops in the Garden," "Fossil Plants of California," and "Alpine Flora of the Sierra Nevada."

Location:
In Tilden Regional Park, at South Park Drive and Wildcat Canyon Road.

Hours and Admission:
Open daily from 10:00 a.m. to 5:00 p.m. Admission free.

For More Information:
East Bay Regional Park District
11500 Skyline Boulevard
Oakland, CA 94619
(510) 531-9300

Berkeley Municipal Rose Garden
Berkeley

It is a place of unique beauty and great tranquility. It would not smell as sweet in any other place or any other city because it does belong to Berkeley. — ALAN GOLDFARB

SURROUNDED by the scent and color of 4,000 roses on a cool morning, the Berkeley hills and the sun rising behind you, San Francisco Bay and the Golden Gate Bridge breaking through the mist before you—it doesn't get much better than this!

Built in an amphitheater, the garden's rose beds rise in a series of tiers, each one planted with a particular color. The rows begin at the lower level with white varieties like Iceberg and Sweet Afton. Just above grow light pinks like Cherry Vanilla and Pristine. Pale pink moves into light and brighter yellows like the buttery Sunflare and Pot o' Gold. Your eye sweeps up through bicolored roses, like the fragrant apricot-orange Sundowner and the orange-red Fragrant Cloud, to the medium-red hybrid teas like Keepsake and Electron. The top row glows with the ruby-red flowers of American Pride and Precious Platinum. A 220-foot pergola crowns the whole with, appropriately enough, the multicolored climber Joseph's Coat.

Blooming season lasts from

Dew-covered rose.

mid-May until October; but if you visit in late spring or early summer, you'll see the garden at its peak.

Location:
At Euclid Avenue and Bayview Place in Berkeley.

Hours and Admission:
Open daily from sunrise to sunset. Admission free.

For More Information:
Berkeley Municipal Rose Garden
City of Berkeley Department of Parks
201 University Avenue
Berkeley, CA 94720
(510) 644-6530

University of California, Berkeley Botanical Garden

Berkeley

The Botanical Garden begins its second century with an important charge—to help protect global biodiversity by generating greater public interest in plants. I invite you to join us.

— DR. ROBERT ORNDUFF, DIRECTOR, BOTANICAL GARDEN

 HIRTY-THREE acres of gardens sprawl out before you, offering a variety of possibilities. Will it be the lush cool shade of the Mather Redwood Grove across the road to your right; the exotic beauty of cacti, aloes, and ice plants on sunny hillsides to your left; or the North American section straight ahead? Your choice will depend on

Strawberry Creek trickles through the garden.

the time of year, the weather, and your whim of the moment. Obviously, this is a garden to visit often and let yourself be swept along with the change of seasons and cycles of life.

For the most part, the 12,000 plant species cluster according to their native regions. Strawberry Creek trickles through the center of the gardens, with little waterfalls, pools, and ferns along its route. On clear days you can see across San Francisco Bay to the city of San Francisco gleaming in the distance.

Garden Highlights

Californian Section

Arranged geographically or by habitat, flowers and plants include many rare, endangered, and interesting California natives. Giant coreopsis (*Coreopsis gigantea*) from Santa Rosa Island blooms golden in spring next to island alum root (*Heuchera maxima*) from Santa Cruz Island. Look for the delicate orange-centered yellow flowers of the tree poppy (*Dendromecon rigida*) from San Miguel Island. An oak knoll blooms in spring with over 300 types of wild California bulbs—everything from colorful brodiaeas to lilies.

Mather Redwood Grove

A cool, shady forest awaits you in Mather Redwood Grove—five acres of towering redwoods, wild flowers, ferns, and shrubs.

Southern African

Lilies, ice plants, euphorbias, and aloes run rampant on a sunny hillside. Time your visit for spring to enjoy the rich orange, red, and magenta flowers.

New World Desert

Concentrating on plants from North and Central America, this section features the oldest specimens in the gardens, some of them dating back to the 1930s. In spring, cacti put forth their spectacular flowers-within-a-flower blossoms. Be sure to look for *Trichocereus litoralis* from Chile and *T. schickendantzii*, whose creamy white blooms beg for a second look.

Asian/Japanese Pool

This pond—filled with water lilies and surrounded by colorful rhododendrons, purplish blue irises, and lush green foliage— offers a visual feast and an emotional respite from the outside world. Stone lanterns add to the serenity as a multitiered waterfall gently splashes in the background. Stones by the pool came from Japan as part of a display for the 1939 International Exposition. Colorful koi once swam in the pool until a number of hungry cormorants put an end to that.

The delicate reedlike *Maesa japonica* from Japan's Okinawa prefecture grows throughout this section. Redwoods, tall rhododendrons, Monterey pines, and coast live oaks create a cool, shady microclimate.

Australian/New Zealand

Eucalyptus trees, numerous strange-looking proteas, and ever-green podocarps thrive along with red-flowering callistemon and hardy melaleuca.

South American

A stately Santa Lucia fir (*Abies bracteata*) guards this section, its long, drooping limbs thick with needles. Pink, red, purple, and magenta fuchsias grow well, too, along with monkey puzzle and Antarctic beech trees.

Mediterranean/European

European trees form an Old World woodland. North American garden perennials complement a rock garden of sempervivums.

North American

Eastern species of plants and trees create a touch of color in the fall as the leaves turn red, orange, and yellow. Fruit trees intermingle with birches and eastern oaks.

Mesoamerican

Mexican pines and oaks clustered at the entrance to the gardens include a Mexican handflower tree.

Palms and Cycads

Lawson cypress (*Chamaecyparis lawsoniana*) and Himalayan deodar cedar (*Cedrus deodara*) line the way to the palms and cycads. The path also leads to the Tropical House, where pale pink anthuriums bloom next to a splashing fountain. Lush tropical flowers, foliage, and spices (including cinnamon) surround you on three sides.

Special-Interest Gardens

The Garden of Old Roses features cultivars from the 1800s and early 1900s. While the Garden of Economic Plants focuses on plants sold as food, dye, and fiber, the Western Herb Garden groups plants used for flavoring, fragrance, and medicine.

An especially interesting section, the Chinese Medicinal Herb Garden, displays plants according to their function in traditional Chinese medicine. You'll see herbs for pacifying the spirit, such as white mulberry (*Morus alba*); radish (*Raphanus sativus*) for removing congestion; and anticancer herbs like strawberry geranium (*Saxifraga stolonifera*), Madagascar periwinkle (*Catharanthus roseus*), and plain old cotton (*Gossypiun arboreum*). You'll even find opium poppies (*Papaver somniferum*)—labeled "astringent herb."

Irises and water lilies highlight the Asian/Japanese Pool.

Greenhouses

The Desert and Rainforest House holds seasonal exhibits of cacti, succulents, and tropical orchids. The Fern and Insectivorous Plant House displays unusual insect-eating plants along with ferns from around the world.

Birds

Birds are as diverse as the plants. Residents include brown and rufous-sided towhees, dark-eyed juncos, common flickers, hairy and downy woodpeckers, Anna's hummingbirds, black phoebes, scrub and Steller jays, chestnut-backed chickadees, red-breasted nuthatches, wrentits, California thrashers, robins, Hutton's vireos, mourning doves, American kestrels, turkey vultures, red-tailed and Cooper's hawks, and purple, house, and American gold finches.

From April through September, you're likely to encounter rufous hummingbirds, red-breasted sapsuckers, western tanagers, black-headed grosbeaks, and Audubon's, Townsend's, orange-crowned, Wilson's, and yellow warblers.

In August, in the California section, you may encounter a covey of California quail—mom, dad, and a brood of chicks. The chicks I saw were no bigger than mice. While protective, these birds are somewhat accustomed to people and will let you approach within ten feet or so. Mom usually leads the way, with dad bringing up the rear.

Butterflies

In spring, you'll find checkerspots in the damper areas of the gardens and Sara orange-tips (*Anthocharis sara*) in open spaces near wild mustard. Summer brings out the brownish orange fritillaries, brownish gray satyrs (look in the trees), and yellowish alfalfa butterflies (or sulphurs) In fall, look for the cocoons of native silk moths on cherry and plum trees, wild cherry, and wild lilac. Watch for mourning cloaks on warm days in the winter. Check the Western Herb Garden for the yellow and black anise swallowtail (*Papilio zelicaon*), where the larvae eat fennel and cow parsnip and the adults sip nectar from mint and penstemon.

Tours and Programs

Docents lead free public tours every Saturday and Sunday at 1:30 p.m. A wide range of special programs, weekend classes, and workshops for adults and children ranges from a general overview of the major garden areas to classes in basic botany to a survey course (by special arrangement) in the basic plants and principles of Chinese traditional medicine.

Location:
At North Canyon Road and Centennial Drive on the University of California, Berkeley campus.

Hours and Admission:
Open daily from 9:00 a.m. to 4:45 p.m.; closed December 25. Admission free.

For More Information:
University of California, Berkeley
Botanical Garden
Centennial Drive at Strawberry Canyon
University of California, Berkeley
Berkeley, CA 94720
(510) 642-3343

Blake Garden

Kensington

*For the mind disturbed, the still beauty of
dawn is nature's finest balm.*

— EDWIN WAY TEALE

s I walked up to the little pool, the sun broke
through the gray morning mist, much to the delight
of the water lilies. They opened so fast you could
practically see their petals moving. Blake Garden is
like that—a modest and quiet place where subtle natural occur-
rences surprise and delight you.

Walkways lead past enormous dark green cypress trees
(*Cupressus macrocarpa*) to lush-leaved magnolias (*Magnolia
delavayi*) standing watch over purple and white lily of the Nile
(*Agapanthus orientalis*) and creeping buttercup (*Ranunculus
repens*). You meander past formal pools lined with magnolias
through a Yellow (or Morning) Garden, towering redwoods
(*Sequoia sempervirens*), a Pink (or Evening) Garden, and a
rhododendron dell to overlook San Francisco Bay with the
Golden Gate Bridge in the distance.

The garden claims the 30-year-old pair of *Eucryphia x
nymansensis* Mt. Usher in front of Blake House as two of the best
specimens in the United States. Visit the garden in August to see
the trees in full flower.

Notable birds include the green heron (*Butorides striatus*),
ruby-crowned kinglet (*Regulus calendula*), red-shafted flicker
(*Colaptes auratus*), and red-breasted sapsucker (*Sphyrapicus
ruber*). Red-tailed and sharp-shinned hawks have been spotted.
If you're lucky, you may also see a rufous hummingbird
(*Selasphorus rufus*) sipping water in mid-flight from the fine
spray of a sprinkler.

Location:
At 70 Rincon Road in the hills above Kensington.

Hours and Admission:
Open weekdays from 8:00 a.m. to 4:30 p.m.; closed holidays and weekends. Admission free.

For More Information:
Department of Landscape Architecture
College of Environmental Design
University of California
Berkeley, CA 94720
(510) 524-2449

Micke Grove Park Japanese Garden
Lodi

Cherry blossoms—
lights
of years past. – BASHO

 ATHWAYS and stepping-stones take you through a lovely garden designed by Nagao Sakurai, superintendent of the Imperial Palace Garden in Tokyo for 20 years. A small rose garden nearby comes into full bloom in early summer.

The garden runs the spectrum from monochromatic subtlety to loud, boisterous color. Silvery water splashes over gray and black stones; a stone pagoda nestles under birch trees and alders; pines and junipers provide patches of severe dark green. Sixty cherry trees create a delightful contrast with pale pink clouds of flowers in spring. Hundreds of camel-

Rose garden.

lias bloom bright red to soft pink in winter. Azaleas burst forth in early spring. In fall, the golden yellow colors of ginkgo trees combine with the rich reds of Japanese maples. Red, orange, black, and white koi swim lazily in a pond below a red-trimmed bridge year round.

Location:
In Micke Grove Park on West Eight Mile Road in Lodi.

Hours and Admission:
Open weekdays from 9:00 a.m. to 3:45 p.m., weekends 9:00 a.m. to 2:00 p.m. Vehicle entrance fee to Micke Grove Park.

For More Information:
Micke Grove Park
San Joaquin County Department of Parks and Recreation
4520 W. Eight Mile Road
Stockton, CA 95209
(209) 953-8800 or (209) 331-7400

Capitol Park
Sacramento

He who plants a tree
Plants a hope. — LUCY LARCOM

 XTENSIVE collections of trees, camellias, desert plants, and roses sprawl over 40 acres around California's state capitol building. A weeping Japanese red pine (*Pinus densiflora*) and a star magnolia (*Magnolia stellata*) flank the entrance to the capitol building. Pepper trees, Mexican and California fan palms, and jacarandas (with their profusion of purple flowers) enhance the State Library and Courts Building.

Trees in the Memorial Grove east of the capitol building were transplanted from Southern battlefields in memory of those who gave their lives during the Civil War. Signs link trees to their former locations. A black locust (*Rabinia pseudoacacia*) stands next to several varieties of elm, and nearby grows an eastern flowering dogwood (*Cornus florida*). This is an especially beautiful place to visit in autumn when the leaves turn color.

Capitol Park rose garden.

Slightly north of the Memorial Grove, the Camellia Grove presents more than 300 varieties of camellias in bloom from February through March.

Eight hundred roses bloom throughout the summer in the far eastern section of the park. From the rose garden you can see more than 50 kinds of trees, including pine, fir, maple, eucalyptus, cypress, and chestnut. Spring blooms highlight a small cactus garden.

To fully appreciate the scope of this park, pick up a copy of the "Capitol Park Tree Tour," a free brochure available in the State Capitol Museum Tour office. The pamphlet suggests three different walks through the park and outlines what types of trees grow where.

Location:
Bounded by 9th, 15th, N, and L streets in downtown Sacramento.

Hours and Admission:
Open daily from dawn to dusk. Admission free.

For More Information:
Department of General Services
Buildings and Grounds Division
State of California
915 Capitol Mall
Sacramento, CA 95814
(916) 324-0333

Arboretum of the University of California, Davis

Davis

The place is so big you can't see everything, so each time I come here I concentrate on a small section. Maybe when I'm an old lady I'll have seen it all!   — GARDEN VISITOR

 O TOUR the entire arboretum requires a serious commitment to walking. The garden's 100 acres hug the banks of Putah Creek, which makes it long and narrow. The creek, however, makes the walk more interesting, since the water attracts herons and egrets, waterfowl, and dragonflies. So in addition to enjoying the trees, plants, and flowers (1,600 different kinds), there's always a possibility of seeing a heron swoop in or a couple of ducks nesting along the creek bank.

Garden Highlights

Trees

The 15-acre Peter J. Shields Oak Grove contains 80 species of oaks from around the world. Pick up a copy of the self-guided tour booklet that tells you about each of the trees you're seeing. Well-marked "information stops" correspond to numbered items in the booklet.

The creek bank (once the stagecoach route from Sacramento to San Francisco) bristles with conifers such as juniper, cedar, pine, and redwood. A grove of eucalyptus contains many different species. Acacias, ranging from low shrubs to tall trees, bloom with fragrant, bright yellow flowers. The Weier Redwood Grove offers a cool respite from the hot Central Valley sun. North coast trees such as California bay and Lawson cypress appear along with Catalina cherry from California's islands.

Demonstration Gardens

The Ruth Risdon Storer Garden features a variety of easy-to-grow, drought-tolerant plants chosen for their interesting textures and year-round color. Rosemary (*Rosmarinus officinalis*), with dark to pale blue flowers, grows near rock rose (*Cistus*) covered with showy flowers in spring and summer. A collection of lavenders includes English, Spanish, and French. Woolly blue-curls (*Trichostema lanatum*) flower from April to June. Garden classics such as Austrian copper rose, damask rose (*Rosa damascena*), globe thistle, bearded iris, and lilac (*Syringa laciniata*) also enhance this garden.

The Carolee Shields White Flower Garden emulates medieval Hindu gardens designed for viewing at night, when the white blossoms would glow in the silvery moonlight. Plants include poet's jasmine (*Jasminum officinale*), whose oils are used in perfumes; woolly lamb's ears (*Stachys byzantina*), whose name perfectly describes the leaves; and matilija poppy, or "fried egg bush" (*Romneya coulteri*), whose petals in late spring and summer resemble crepe silk. Notice the Australian tea tree (*Leptospermum* White Swan), called a tea tree because Captain Cook brewed its leaves to prevent scurvy among his men. A southern magnolia (*Magnolia grandiflora*) adds the charm of deep green leaves and big creamy-white flowers.

Native California drought-tolerant plants in the Mary Wattis Brown Garden ramble along a dry creek bed and around a shady patio. A stunning collection of blue-flowering ceanothus, or California wild lilac, highlights the garden

Birds

Over 130 bird species live at the arboretum. Expect to see mallards and great blue, green-backed, and black-crowned night herons year round. Wood ducks and cinnamon teals nest along Putah Creek. Look for American bitterns from October through April. Swainson's hawks (*Buteo swainsoni*) nest in the area, along with the most common birds of prey, kestrel and Cooper's hawks. You'll see red-tailed hawks, harriers, and turkey vultures just about everywhere.

California quail and ring-necked pheasants (*Phasianus colchicus*) scurry about all year. The burrowing owl is the only owl you'll see here in the daytime; the barn, western screech, and great horned owls come out at night.

Anna's hummingbirds live at the arboretum all year. Rufous and black-chinned hummingbirds migrate through in spring and fall. Northern flickers (*Colaptes auratus*) and Nuttall's woodpeckers (*Picoides nuttallii*) flit regularly through the valley oaks (*Quercus lobata*). Belted kingfishers live along the arboretum waterways as do Brewer's and red-winged blackbirds.

Perching birds include swallows that nest around banks, barns, and bridges. Magpies, scrub jays, robins, and mockingbirds abound. Cedar waxwings (*Bombycilla cedrorum*) arrive in winter to feast on the bright red berries of toyon (*Heteromeles arbutifolia*).

Mammals, Reptiles, Amphibians

While 33 species of mammals live at the arboretum, most steer clear of humans. Opossums and ten species of bats rest in hidden nooks and crannies and under bridges. You may see California jackrabbits (*Lepus californicus*) and Audubon's cottontails (*Sylvilagus audubonii*) hopping around the grounds, however—and plenty of California ground squirrels (*Spermophilus beecheyi*).

Chances are extremely slim, but you may encounter the Pacific gopher snake or the western yellowbelly racer (*Coluber constrictor*). The southern alligator lizard (*Gerrhonotus multicarinatus*) lives in the garden as well. Because of the proximity to water, you can also find California toads (*Bufo boreas*), bullfrogs (*Rana catesbeiana*), and turtles.

Tours

Three self-guided tour books walk you through the Carolee Shields White Flower Garden, the Ruth Risdon Storer Garden, and the Peter J. Shields Oak Grove. Another publication, "Native California Plants," suggests two different walks through the arboretum. An excellent reference with clearly drawn sketches, the booklet explains the various plants you'll see, where they

Winding pathway at U.C. Davis Arboretum.

come from, and how they were used by early natives.

Regular guided tours begin at 2:00 p.m. on Sundays. They follow themes such as "Plants of the American Deserts," "The Acacia Collection," "California Native Plants," "The Conifer Collection," "Redwoods and Manzanitas," and more. Guided tours of the Storer and Shields gardens concentrate on the use of drought-tolerant flowering perennials. Arrange for group tours by calling (916) 752-4880.

Location:
Off Interstate 80's UC Davis exit, past the Visitor Information kiosk on Old Davis Road and left on La Rue Road.

Hours and Admission:
Open daily from sunrise to sunset. Admission free.

For More Information:
Friends of the Davis Arboretum
University of California
Davis, CA 95616
(916) 752-2498

Luther Burbank Home and Memorial Gardens

Santa Rosa

I firmly believe, from what I have seen, that this is the chosen spot of all this earth as far as Nature is concerned.   — LUTHER BURBANK

 N ARCHED white trellis frames your first view of Luther Burbank's home and carriage house. Brick walkways lead you through the small gardens beyond. The squawking of scrub jays breaks the morning calm.

Luther Burbank, known as the "plant wizard," conducted his horticultural experiments on these four acres. Improving the quality of plants by mass breeding and selection, he introduced such favorites as the Burbank potato (now known as the Idaho baker), the Satsuma plum, the royal walnut, and, of course, the Shasta daisy.

Burbank aimed 53 years of plant-breeding toward increasing the world's food supply by improving plant quality. His experiments yielded more than 200 new variations of fruit, hundreds of flowers, and more than 800 new varieties of plants.

Foxgloves bloom in spring.

The garden behind the home and carriage house contains a wide selection of trees, making this a pleasant destination on a hot California afternoon. Look for the hybrid southern magnolia (*Magnolia grandiflora* St. Mary), California live oak (*Quercus agrifolia*), a pair of *ginkgo biloba* trees, Italian buckthorn (*Rhamni alaternus argento variegata*), and Indian haw-thorn (*Raphiolepsis indica rosea*).

You can tour the home between April 4 and October 14, Wednesday through Sunday from 10:00 a.m. to 3:30 p.m.

Location:
On Sonoma Avenue in Santa Rosa.

Hours and Admission:
Open daily from 8:00 a.m. to 7:00 p.m. Admission free.

For More Information:
Luther Burbank Home and Memorial Gardens
P.O. Box 1678
Santa Rosa, CA 95402
(707) 524-5445

Kruse Rhododendron State Reserve Plantation
Jenner

*A sound arises out of the earth—
a singing, a friendliness.*   — CEDRIC WRIGHT

S YOU WALK through this cool, silent rhododendron forest, foggy mists swirling around you, you feel as if the primeval setting has been here forever. It hasn't.

A major forest fire destroyed what was once a thick forest of redwood, eucalyptus, tanbark oak, and Douglas fir, making room for the rhododendrons to take hold and thrive. Growing up to 14 feet in height, the dark green shrubs produce flowers that range from rose pink to rose purple. Rarely will you see a cream-colored or white flower.

Visit in April, when the 317 acres of California rhododendron

(*Rhododendron macrophyllum*) reach their peak of color. Five miles of fern-lined hiking trails lead throughout the reserve.

Location:
Ten miles north of Fort Ross and east of Highway 1, off Kruse Ranch Road in Salt Point State Park.

Hours and Admission:
Open daily from dawn to dusk. Admission free.

Rhododendron blossom.

For More Information:
Department of State Parks
25050 Coast Highway 1
Jenner, CA 94550
(707) 865-2391

Mendocino Coast Botanical Gardens
Fort Bragg

Commonly we stride through the out-of-doors too swiftly to see more than the most obvious and prominent things. For observing nature, the best pace is a snail's pace.

— EDWIN WAY TEALE

EXTRAORDINARY gardens—made even more extraordinary by their location—perch high on a headland along the Mendocino coast. A visit takes you from meticulously cared-for plantings near the main entrance to a forest of rhododendrons, ferns, and pines and out to a stunning seaside bluff. California gray whales migrate offshore, Steller sea lions bask on the rocks, and waves crash continually. Tamed at the front gate, nature gets wilder the farther into the gardens you go.

Garden Highlights

Specialized Gardens

The more civilized areas near the entrance feature sections of perennials, roses, ivies, camellias, heathers, succulents, Mediterranean plants, and dwarf conifers. Individual garden beds and mounds—like islands in a sea of lawn—invite you to follow paths that twist and turn and double back.

The perennial garden peaks in mid-summer as matilija poppies, reddish purple liatris, dahlias, agapanthus, and penstemons (pale pink to rosy purple) come into full bloom. The cinnamon-colored leaves of Japanese maples (*Acer palmatum*) complement a carefully tended dwarf conifer collection. Selections include deodar cedar (*Cedrus deodara*), Colorado spruce (*Picea pungens*), and dwarf Norway spruce (*P. abies*).

Old roses climb and ramble through a small Heritage Rose Garden. Wild roses, native California ceanothus, manzanita, and various forms of lavender fill the Mediterranean Climate Garden nearby. Heather (*Calluna*) blooms from July to December in the Heather Garden, its cool green leaves turning to rust in the fall. An open-air lath Ivy House contains the largest collection of ivy in the United States—over 400 varieties donated by the American Ivy Association.

Rhododendrons

Rhododendrons star in April and May, when you're never far from the treelike bushes laden with shades of pure white to dark purple. Basking in dappled sunlight under tanbark oaks, they surprise you with color wherever you look. California's native rhododendrons (*R. macrophyllum* and *R. occidentale*) have grown here for thousands of years and are well represented. Numerous hybrids include a Fort Bragg variety called Noyo Chief.

Nature Trails

Paths lead out of the more formal gardens to the less tended Pine Forest Trail, Canyon Rim Trail, and Fern Canyon Trail. Pacific

The bluffs at Mendocino Coast Botanical Gardens.

wax myrtles (*Myrica californica*), tanbark oaks, Monterey cypresses, shore pines (*Pinus contorta*), Bishop pines (*P. muricata*), alders, and redwoods shelter the ground from sun and wind. The trees also act as a natural drip irrigation system; moisture from the fog condenses on the leaves and then slowly drips onto the ferns, lilies, and fuchsias below. Paths wind over bridges and beside Digger and Schoefer creeks, past wild ginger, wild mushrooms (in fall), daylilies, Japanese irises (*Iris ensata*), and sword ferns.

You suddenly find yourself out on a headland, where you can gaze up and down the Mendocino coast to see the waves pounding the rocky shoreline. California poppies dot the grassy meadow in spring, along with ice plant and red hot poker (*Kniphofia uvaria*). Look for the endangered Mendocino coast paintbrush (*Castilleja latifolia mendocinensis*), a wild flower found only in Mendocino County.

Birds

The garden's three distinct areas (open formal plantings, fern canyons, and coastal bluffs) host a wide variety of bird life.

Anna's and Allen's hummingbirds frequent the perennial gardens, while woodpeckers, red-breasted sapsuckers, and northern flickers swoop through the pine and oak forests. Along the coastal bluffs you can see cormorants, California quail, robins, and black oystercatchers (*Haematopus bachmani*). Birders can also expect brown pelicans (*Pelecanus occidentalis*), black scoters, ospreys, black-shouldered kites (*Elanus caeruleus*), chestnut-backed chickadees, bushtits, cedar waxwings, and various warblers, sparrows, and finches.

Mammals and Amphibians

Though seldom seen by human visitors, mammals in the gardens include deer, raccoons, squirrels, rabbits, opossums, chipmunks, and skunks. California gray whales (*Eschrichtius robustus*) migrate past the headlands—sometimes but a half-mile away—from December to January and again from February to May.

Along the creeks and near the bog you may see the two salamanders native to the area—the Northwestern salamander (*Ambystoma gracile*) and the black (with gray or green markings) salamander (*Aneides flavipunctatus*).

Tours

The local Audubon Society conducts bird walks through the gardens every Wednesday at 10:00 a.m.

Location:
Two miles south of Fort Bragg and six miles north of Mendocino on Highway 1.

Hours and Admission:
Open daily from 9:00 a.m. to 5:00 p.m. March through October; daily from 10:00 a.m. to 4:00 p.m. the rest of the year. Closed Thanksgiving, December 25, and January 1. Admission fee.

For More Information:
Mendocino Coast Botanical Gardens
18220 N. Highway 1
P.O. Box 1143
Fort Bragg, CA 95437
(707) 964-4352

Azalea State Reserve
Arcata

We do not weave the web of life,
We are merely a strand in it.
Whatever we do to the web,
We do to ourselves....   — CHIEF SEATTLE

ARROW DIRT PATHS wind around and through 30 acres of wild western azaleas (*Rhododendron occidentale*). The densely packed stands of pale pink flowers reach their peak from May through June. Blue-flowering ceanothus provides a pleasing contrast to the azaleas. Watch your feet as you walk—you don't want to step on one of the large slugs that cross the paths from time to time. The little critters (*Ariolimax columbianus*) can reach up to six inches in size!

Location:
On the north side of the Mad River, east of Highway 101 on North Bank Road.

Hours and Admission:
Open daily from sunrise to sunset. Admission free.

For More Information:
Azalea Reserve
California State Parks
600A West Clark
Eureka, CA 95501
(707) 677-3570

Western azaleas in bloom.

DeAnza College Environmental Study Area

Cupertino

SIX hundred plants representing 350 species pack this tiny 1.5-acre garden. Call ahead to join a student-led tour. Open the first Saturday of every month from noon to 4:00 p.m. Admission free. For more information, contact DeAnza College Environmental Study Area, Stelling and McClellan Roads, Cupertino, CA 95014. Or call (408) 996-4525.

Elizabeth F. Gamble Garden Center

Palo Alto

AN interesting combination of formal and working gardens surround a 1902 mansion. To the right of the house, fronted by a couple of beautiful magnolia trees, you walk through a Cherry Allee to a little rose garden where white Iceberg roses enclose a circular patch of lawn. The Wisteria Garden and a small water-lily pond lie directly behind the mansion. Nearby, the Woodland Garden leads you out to the working beds.

A few scarecrows guard the working gardens' herbs, vegetables, and ornamental flowers. Long rows of dahlias grow next to rows of lilies, cosmos, and a variety of salvias. Scrub jays, squirrels, robins, and painted lady butterflies abound. Open daily from dawn to dusk. Admission free. For more information, contact the Elizabeth F. Gamble Garden Center, 1431 Waverley Street, Palo Alto, CA 94301. Or call (415) 329-1356.

Sunset Publishing Company
Menlo Park

EVER-CHANGING beds of bulbs and annuals highlight *Sunset* magazine's ten-acre showplace. Plants, trees, and flowers appear geographically, in sections representing Southern California's

Drought-tolerant succulent.

cacti and succulents or the Pacific Coast's rhododendrons and azaleas. Sunset offers free tours of the gardens, test kitchens, and offices at 10.30 a.m. and 2:30 p.m. Groups of eight or more should call for reservations. Open weekdays from 9:00 a.m. to 4:30 p.m. Admission free. For more information, contact Sunset Publishing Company, 80 Willow Road, Menlo Park, CA 94025-3691. Or call (415) 321-3600.

San Mateo Arboretum
San Mateo

WITH the exception of rhododendrons and azaleas, very few flowers grow here. This is an arboretum in the truest sense of the word, since the emphasis is on trees. The impressive collection includes a multitrunked Spanish fir (*Abies pinsapo*), coast live and valley oaks, dawn redwoods, and Lawson's cypress. The arboretum aims to create "a haven of beauty and learning within an urban environment" by continually improving, developing, and changing. Open to view year round. Admission free. For more information, contact the San Mateo Arboretum Society, P.O. Box 1523, San Mateo, CA 94401. Or call (415) 574-8338.

San Jose Rose Garden
San Jose

THIS rose garden packs more than 7,500 plants into 5.5 acres. Arranged symmetrically, the collection includes climbing roses, miniatures, hybrids, and teas. Visit in May and June to witness the peak blooming period. Open daily from 8:00 a.m. to half an hour before sunset. Admission free. For more information, contact the Municipal Rose Gardens, Naglee Avenue at Dana Street, San Jose, CA 95126. Or call (408) 287-0698.

Japanese Gardens
Hayward

A SMALL lake and teahouse highlight 3.25 acres of traditional Japanese gardens. Open daily from 10:00 a.m. to 4:00 p.m. Admission free. For more information, contact Japanese Gardens, 22372 N. Third Street, Hayward, CA. Or call (510) 881-6715.

Rod McLellan Company Acres of Orchids
South San Francisco

SOMETHING'S always blooming at this huge commercial orchid nursery. Time your visit for fall, winter, or early spring to see cymbidiums and lady slippers, spring and fall to see the cattleya peak. The Visitors' Center, open daily from 8:00 a.m. to 5:00 p.m., offers tours at 10:30 a.m. and 1:30 p.m. Admission free. For more information, contact the Rod McLellan Company, Acres of Orchids, 1450 El Camino Real, South San Francisco, CA 94080. Or call (415) 871-5655.

Lombard Street
San Francisco

KNOWN as "the crookedest street in San Francisco," Lombard (between Hyde and Leavenworth) zigzags downhill through a garden of colorful hydrangea bushes. Open to view year round.

Golden Gate Park
Fuchsia Garden
San Francisco

EAST of the Conservatory of Flowers behind John McLaren House, tall cypress trees shade 3,000 fuchsia plants of 400 varieties. The climate of mist and fog perfectly suits these beautiful flowers. Visit in July and August to see the blossoms at their best. Open to view year round.

Queen Wilhelmina
Tulip Garden and Windmill
San Francisco

MONTEREY cypress trees tower over formal tulip beds and Iceland poppies in the northwest corner of Golden Gate Park, at the intersection of Great Highway and Kennedy Drive. Open to view year round, but look for the best show in April.

Golden Gate Park
Rose Garden
San Francisco

OVER 75 varieties of roses grow in this small garden, including grandifloras, climbers, hybrid teas, and old roses. Located east of Stow Lake on the north side of Kennedy Drive, the garden peaks in May. Open to view year round.

Morcom Amphitheater of Roses
Oakland

LOOKING much like an Italian Renaissance garden, Morcom Amphitheater of Roses showcases 8,000 rose bushes (500 varieties) in a setting of curving colonnades and beautifully crafted stonemasonry and ironwork. Redwoods, pines, cedars, and junipers form a backdrop while a waterfall provides a secondary focal point. Because the gardens are somewhat shaded, the flowers begin blooming a little later than normal, peaking from May through September. Located at 700 Jean Street. Open daily from dawn to dusk. Admission free. To prearrange a guided group tour, call (510) 273-3151. For more information, contact Morcom Amphitheater of Roses, Oakland Office of Parks and Recreation, 1520 Lakeside Drive, Oakland, CA 94612. Or call (510) 658-0731.

Oakland Museum and Gardens
Oakland

THIS elaborately designed garden consists of three levels of plantings on terraces and platforms above the street. Geraniums and poppies, olive and pear trees decorate a number of platforms for viewing Lake Merritt. Docent-led weekday tours convene at gallery information desks on each level at 2:00 p.m. Open Wednesday through Saturday from 10:00 a.m. to 5:00 p.m; Sunday noon to 7:00 p.m. Closed Monday, Tuesday, July 4, Thanksgiving, December 25, and January 1. Admission free. For more information, contact Oakland Museum and Gardens, 1000 Oak Street, Oakland, CA 94607. Or call (510) 834-2413.

Kaiser Center Roof Garden
Oakland

A LOFTY garden—built on the roof of the 28-story Kaiser Center—offers flower beds, a reflecting pool, pathways, and a stupendous view of the surrounding area. You can reach the garden from the third floor of the Mall Shop Building or from the Kaiser Center Garage. Open Monday through Saturday from 7:00 a.m. to 7:00 p.m. Admission free. For more information, contact Kaiser Center Roof Garden, 300 Lakeside Drive, Suite 2685, Oakland, CA 94643. Or call (510) 271-6100.

Daffodil Hill
Volcano

TUCKED away in gold rush country, three miles north of Volcano, a six-acre garden blooms with 250,000 daffodils, narcissus, tulips, and jonquils every spring. The flowers have been maintained since their original planting in the 1850s. Daffodils spring up all over the place during the short blooming season—late March to mid-April. Open daily mid-March to mid-April from 9:00 a.m. to 5:00 p.m. Admission free. For more information, contact Daffodil Hill, 18310 Ram's Horn Grade, Volcano, CA. Or call (209) 296-7048.

Esther Baker Memorial Garden
Auburn

THE Auburn Garden Club planted this Japanese garden in 1973 following a design by Ray Yamasaki. Birds enjoy a traditional Japanese water basin. Open Tuesday through Thursday from 10:00 a.m. to 8:00 p.m., Friday to 6:00 p.m., and Saturday to 5:00 p.m. Admission free. For more information, contact Esther Baker Memorial Garden, Auburn-Placer Library, 350 Nevada Street, Auburn, CA 95603. Or call (916) 889-4111.